Blogging

JILL WALKER RETTBERG

polity

First published in 2008 by Polity Press
Reprinted 2009

Polity Press
65 Bridge Street
Cambridge CB2 1UR, UK

Polity Press
350 Main Street
Malden, MA 02148, USA

ISBN-13: 978-0-7456-4133-1
ISBN-13: 978-0-7456-4134-8(pb)

A catalogue record for this book is available from the British Library.

Typeset in 10.25 on 13 pt FF Scala
by Servis Filmsetting Ltd, Stockport, Cheshire
Printed and bound in Great Britain by the MPG Books Group

Text design by Peter Ducker

For further information on Polity, visit our website: www.polity.co.uk

Contents

Acknowledgements

Without the constant conversations with the readers of my blog and with other bloggers, and the inspiration of reading blogs throughout the blogosphere, this book wouldn't have existed. Thanks also to Blogger.com, for making me aware that anyone, even I, could easily make a blog – that opened new worlds to me.

While writing this book I've had the support of my colleagues at the University of Bergen, particularly the humanistic informatics group, and I would like to thank everyone there for years of conversations and ideas. I also spent a month at the University of Western Australia, finishing the manuscript while a guest researcher at the Department of Communication Studies. Tama Leaver (of tamaleaver.net) was especially helpful during my stay in Perth, reading most of the chapters and making many valuable suggestions for additions and reorganisations. In addition, I received useful comments from Ingeborg Kleppe at the Norwegian School of Economics and Business Administration.

My editor at Polity Press, Andrea Drugan, has been an inspiration and support throughout the process of writing this book, from working out the synopsis to finishing the manuscript. Her feedback has always been rapid and helpful. I've also appreciated the feedback I've received from the reviewers, which has helped me to make many improvements to the manuscript.

Many thanks are due to Heather B. Armstrong, Jason Kottke, and Markos Moulitsas for permission to reprint screenshots from their blogs. Thank you also to Google for permission to reprint screenshots from the Blogger.com blogging interface, and to the Rand Corporation for permission to reprint the diagram from Paul Baran's paper.

And of course, my deeply loving thanks to my family, especially to my daughter Aurora, for giving me such good reasons to step away from the computer, and to my wonderful husband and colleague Scott Rettberg, for suggesting great examples and discussing ideas along the way, for reading the manuscript several times and giving me very useful feedback, for suggesting the megaphone on the cover, and for being a splendid partner in every way.

Introduction

Ten years ago, the word 'blog' didn't exist. Today, mainstream media routinely use the word without bothering to explain it. Weblogs have become part of popular consciousness with a speed that is remarkable by any standard. What is this new form of communication that has so suddenly entered our culture?

I began blogging in October 2000, when I was working on my PhD thesis, and I've been blogging since. Like most bloggers, I learnt about blogging by doing it. Blogging is as much about reading other blogs as about writing your own, and the best way to understand blogging is to immerse yourself in it. However, blogs are also a part of a larger context. They are part of the history of communication and literacy, and emblematic of a shift from uni-directional mass media to participatory media, where viewers and readers become creators of media. Blogs are also part of the history of literature and writing. A path can be traced from early autobiographical writing through diary writing and memoirs up to the confessional and personal diary-style blogs of today (Serfaty 2004). Blogs are part of the current changes in journalism and in marketing. They are part of the growth of social networks like MySpace and Facebook, which in their turn have roots in the social network theory put forward by sociologists in the 1960s and 1970s, as well as in the network structure of the Internet, which was designed around the same period.

Blogs are founded upon the link, building connections between related issues. Blogs are themselves related to many different contexts and can be interpreted from many different disciplines: media studies, the history of technology, sociology, ethnology, literary studies, marketing, journalism and more. Furthermore, blogs can function as a lens with which to see how all these fields have developed up until today, and with which we can understand more about other, related, social media.

The first chapter of this book is an introduction to blogs, explaining how blogs work. We look at three blogs in detail, each of which represents a different kind of blog. We'll then discuss the defining characteristics of blogs, and finally look at the history of blogging.

The next two chapters look at blogging from two broader yet different perspectives. Chapter 2 sees blogging in a historical context, and explores ways in which major cultural shifts, such as the introduction of print, the spread of literacy, and our expanding access to the Internet connect to blogging. It also examines ways in which cultural theories of communication and writing relate to the practice of blogging. In chapter 3, we look at current research on blogs as social arenas, in particular discussing social network theory and considering how social networks like MySpace and Facebook relate to blogs.

The fourth, fifth and sixth chapters of the book deal with different kinds of blogs. Chapter 4 looks at the symbiosis between blogging and journalism. Chapter 5 considers blogs as narratives, and explores the characteristics of blog narratives both in terms of narrative structure and in terms of the uneasy relationships between fiction, self-representation and authenticity. Chapter 6 examines commercial blogging, looking at the ways in which blogs are being used in marketing and by businesses as well as at the way individuals are setting up blogs as small businesses and earning a living from advertising revenue.

Finally, chapter 7 offers speculations on the future of blogging. Blogging has very rapidly become a popular form of writing – will we still blog in twenty years' time, or will other ways of communicating have taken over by then? Will blogging continue to increase the general public's ability to speak back and to be heard? Will it be subsumed by mass media, or change into something else altogether? What are the perils and promises of blogging?

This book contains references to many blogs, as well as to conventional sources. Blogs that are discussed are not generally included in the main bibliography, but are listed separately at the end of the book, along with their URLs at the time of writing or, in the case of blogs that are no longer actively maintained, their URL at the time they were active. However, blogs are by nature an ephemeral form, and some will have changed URLs or shut down completely by the time you read this. If so, I would recommend trying to enter the URL into The Internet Archive's Wayback Machine at http://archive.org. This will usually provide you with search results allowing you to view the blog as it appeared at regular intervals during the period when it was active.

This book aims to be like a blog in that it constantly links to – or refers to – actual examples of what blogs are doing and what bloggers are writing, as well as to more conventional sources such as scholarship on blogs and their context. Being a book, it can also draw upon the strengths of this slower, longer format by providing a context and a sustained discussion that would be difficult in the faster, more fragmentary medium of blogs. But although reading about blogs is valuable for those who wish to gain an overview and to think about the meaning of blogs in today's culture, anyone who really wants to understand blogs will need to start their own blog and to read other blogs. It's easy. If you haven't already tried blogging, give it a go!

CHAPTER ONE

What is a Blog?

To really understand blogs, you need to read them over time. Following a blog is like getting to know someone, or like watching a television series. Because blogging is a cumulative process, most posts presuppose some knowledge of the history of the blog, and they fit into a larger story. There's a very different sense of rhythm and continuity when you follow a blog, or a group of blogs, over time, compared to simply reading a single post that you've found through a search engine or by following a link from another Web site.

In most forms of print publishing, such as newspaper articles, novels or poetry, the author is not in charge of the way the text will look. The text is written in a word processor (or on a typewriter, or by hand) and submitted to an editor who, usually with a staff of designers, determines the layout. Bloggers, on the other hand, choose their own template and often spend considerable time adjusting the way their blogs look and work. A literary critic will rarely see the binding of a book as being important to its literary quality. A blog, however, cannot be read simply for its writing, but will always be seen as the sum of writing, layout, connections and links, and tempo.

The best way of figuring out what a blog is is simply to look at some examples. I've chosen three blogs for us to look at and analyse: a personal, diary-style blog, a political blog and a blog that combines expertise with a personal twist. After examining these blogs, I'll discuss some definitions of blogs and consider how well they suit our examples. One of the most important reasons for the popularity of blogging is that it is extremely easy to do – so, first of all, let's look at the mechanics of blogging and how you do it. If you're already a blogger, you might want to skip ahead to the examples of different kinds of blog: personal blogs, filter blogs and topic-driven blogs.

How to Blog

There are many online services that will let you set up your own blog for free, and that will host your blog for you on their server. Blogger.com was the first major service to do this, and is still one of the most popular blogging sites, but there are many others, including Wordpress.com, Livejournal.com, TypePad.com, as well as many sites that are specific to a particular country or region.

All these sites require you to create a user account. You're then asked to choose a name for your blog and a URL. Sites that offer free hosting for your blog will generally have a fixed domain for all hosted blogs but allow you to choose the first part of the URL. For instance, Blogger.com hosts users' blogs at blogspot.com, so you could choose the URL http://newblog. blogspot.com or http://myfirstblog.blogspot.com, assuming these URLs aren't already taken. If you already have your own domain (mydomain.com, for instance), you can set the blog up to publish to it instead. The next step is to select a template or theme for your blog (see figure 1). Most blogging services have many different templates to choose from. Later, if you like, you can edit your template to make it just the way you want it. Some of these edits are easy to do, but more complex editing requires basic knowledge of HTML and CSS. HTML stands for HyperText Markup Language, and is the code for writing a Web page that can be displayed in a Web browser. For instance, in HTML, you put the tag <p> at the beginning of a paragraph, and the tag </p> at the end of a paragraph. The browser then knows that text between those two tags should be displayed as a separate paragraph rather than just as a long string of text connected to the text that comes before and after. CSS stands for Cascading Style Sheets, and is a way of specifying how the

Figure 1: Selecting a template for your new blog at Blogger.com. (Screenshot taken 6 August 2007)

Web browser should 'style' or present pages that are marked up in HTML. So, for instance, a CSS 'rule' might specify that all paragraphs should have the first line indented. That would override the default of most Web browsers, which doesn't indent the first line, but instead inserts an extra line break between paragraphs. There are numerous tutorials explaining how to tweak the HTML and CSS code for blog templates to adjust them as you wish, but there are also many changes that can be made without diving into the code.

Once you've chosen a template you've created your blog, and you simply need to fill it with content. You're presented with a small empty box for the title of the post, and a larger box for the post itself (see figure 2). When you've written as much as you

Figure 2: Writing a new post at Blogger.com. The title of the blog is at the very top of the page (in this case, it is 'My New Blog'). You enter the title of the post you are writing in the smaller text box and the main content of the post in the large text box. (Screenshot taken 6 August 2007)

want to write, you simply press the 'Publish Post' button (the publish button has different names on different blogging sites) and your words are uploaded to your blog and published on the Internet.

The templates you can choose from when you create a new blog also show the elements that are expected to be included in a blog. Just as a book is expected to have a cover with its title and the name of the author or editor, a blog usually has a number of standard features. The title of the whole blog is usually displayed at the top of the page, often presented in a graphic banner across the top section. Many blogs have taglines as well – subtitles or brief descriptions of the blog. There'll generally be some information about the blogger in one of the upper corners, often with a photo. Many blog hosting sites encourage users to create profiles about themselves, with a photo, some biographical information and links to their blogs. The default templates will then pull in information from the blogger's profile to display on their blog, thus automatically generating this 'about' section. The main content of the blog – the posts, each with its own title – will generally be in the wide central column, and there are often side columns with automatically generated links to older blog posts (the archives), to other blogs the blogger enjoys reading (this list of links is known as a blogroll) and to comments left by users.

In the last few years, blog software has increasingly incorporated RSS as an additional way of publishing. RSS stands for Really Simple Syndication, and is a version of a Web site encoded in a way that allows computers to easily manipulate the content. For instance, an RSS feed of a blog will use codes like <title> and </title> to mark the beginning and end point of the title of an individual post. The content of the post and the name of the post's author will be similarly encoded, as will the date and time it was published. While blog readers can still visit a blog using their Web browser and read it as a Web page (see, for instance, figures 3, 4 and 5), they can also choose to use an RSS reader to read the RSS feed of a blog. One advantage of this is that you can subscribe to a number of blogs and your RSS reader will automatically alert you when they have new posts. Another advantage of RSS is that RSS feeds can be embedded into other Web pages. So for instance, if I have two blogs, one about my research and one for students in a class I am teaching, I could use the RSS feed from my student blog in my research blog, showing just the titles of the latest posts in my student blog in the sidebar of my research blog.

Blogs aren't the only sites that use RSS. Newspapers, discussion forums and photo sharing sites are just some of the kinds of sites that often provide RSS feeds. I can, for instance, subscribe to an RSS feed of recent activity on my Facebook profile, and embed that in my blog. Or I can use the RSS from my blog and feed it into my Facebook profile. Most blogging software can automatically generate RSS feeds with no need for the user to know anything about the code.

Another term one often comes across in discussions of blogs is Web 2.0. This term was put forward by Tim O'Reilly and associates (O'Reilly 2005). The term is meant to characterize a second generation of Web sites. The first wave of Web developers focused largely on publishing content. Web 2.0, on the other hand, develops services that allow users to share their own content and to use the Web as a platform. Examples of Web 2.0 sites are the Wikipedia, YouTube, Flickr and Facebook. All these are services that become valuable because they are being used. Blogs are also seen as part of Web 2.0.

Three Blogs

An immense range of different blogs can be created using simple blogging software. We'll look at three blogs that represent three main styles of blogging: personal or diary-style blogging, filterblogging and topic-driven blogging.

Personal Blogs: Dooce.com

Dooce is one of the most popular personal blogs. Technorati.com is a site that ranks blogs according to how many other blogs link to them, and *Dooce* has been on Technorati's list of the hundred most popular blogs for several years. 'Dooce' is both the title of the blog and a pseudonym for its author, Heather B. Armstrong. Dooce rose to notoriety as one of the first bloggers to be fired from her job because of things she had written on her blog. In fact, the term 'to be dooced', is listed in UrbanDictionary.com as meaning: 'To be fired from your job because of the contents of your weblog.' These days, Dooce's blog mostly contains droll or satirical stories about life as the mother of a young child, along with photographs, often of her dog or her daughter.

Figure 3: Screenshot of Heather B. Armstrong's blog, Dooce.com (taken 5 August 2007). The most recent post is a letter styled to the blogger's daughter, Leta, on the day she turns forty-two months old.

The basic layout of Dooce.com has remained fairly stable for the last few years, but the colour scheme and banner image across the top of the screen are regularly changed. Dooce is, after all, a designer. As you can see in figure 3, the blog has a large central area for the main content of the site, the posts. There is a simple navigation bar across the top with icons linked to her photos, a link from the small photo of the author to a page with more information about her, and there are ads in narrow columns on the left- and right-hand sides.

Most blogs have a small section in an upper corner that explains who the blogger is or what the blog is about. Sometimes there'll be a photograph of the blogger as well, and often a link to an 'About' page where the blogger explains the purpose and history of the blog, or describes her- or himself. Most blog templates have these features built in, and they will often fetch this information from the blogger's profile or from a form the blogger fills out. Like most blogs, Dooce.com has a link to an 'About' page, where Dooce explains who she is and some of the history of the blog. Here she writes briefly about being fired:

> I started this Web site in February 2001. A year later I was fired from my job for this Web site because I had written stories that included people in my workplace. My advice to you is BE YE NOT SO STUPID. Never write about work on the Internet unless your boss knows and sanctions the fact that YOU ARE WRITING ABOUT WORK ON THE INTERNET.

Yet Dooce seems to have done very well for herself after being fired. Reading the blog entries that led up to her being fired (they're all still online), it's clear that she hated her job as a Web designer in a dot com startup. Today she runs her own Web design business, looks after her daughter, and makes a reasonable income from ads on her very popular blog.

In the first years of blogging, there were no ads. Dooce's blog shows the path towards a commercialization – or, as many bloggers say, the monetization – of blogging. She introduced text ads, like the ones seen in her blog's right-hand column, in 2004, and graphical ads, like the large ad on the left, in 2005. By 2006, Dooce and her husband reported that 'The monthly checks [from the advertisers] add up to a "comfortable enough middle class to upper-middle class income" ' (*Salt Lake Tribune*, October 14, 2006).

Dooce's primary subject is her life. Her blog is a diary that is open to the public. Of course, Dooce doesn't blog everything that happens to her – this is not a secret diary but a diary deliberately written to be shared. Posts are written with care and wit, and are clearly edited before they are published.

Most bloggers who use their blogs as personal diaries do so less publicly than Dooce. Often diarists belong to Web rings linking diaries together, or they write on social sites like LiveJournal, where they can set up friendlists and share sections of their diaries with specified friends or groups of friends. In these cases, the blog is often only meant as a way of communicating with close friends. Dooce's posts don't document every aspect of her life, as a private diary might. Instead, they present slices of her life, episodes and anecdotes that give readers a strong feeling of knowing the blogger, but that also keep many secrets. This is the aspect of blogging that Viviane Serfaty refers to as the veil of the screen (Serfaty 2004: 13–14). She argues that online diarists and bloggers use their writing as a mirror that allows them to see themselves more clearly and to construct themselves as subjects in a digital society, but also as a veil that will always conceal much of their lives from their readers. We'll return to the ways bloggers both reveal and hide their lives from their readers in chapter 5.

Filter Blogs: Kottke.org

Unlike diary-style blogs, filter blogs don't log the blogger's offline life but record his or her experiences and finds on the Web. Jorn Barger's *Robot Wisdom* was one of the first examples of a filter blog, being simply a list of links with no commentary. Most weblogs do, however, provide some commentary in addition to simply linking. Today's filter blogs range from the popular *Boing Boing*, which provides news on bizarre Web finds, to *Metafilter*, a group blog where members post links to interesting Web sites, to personal sites like Rebecca Blood's *Rebecca's Pocket* or Jason Kottke's Kottke.org. While personal blogs like *Dooce* focus mostly on the life of the blogger, filter blogs filter the Web from the blogger's own point of view. There are often dominant topics, but these may shift as the blogger's interests change over time.

Jason Kottke is a Web designer who has been blogging since 1998 at the URL kottke.org. His blog is known for its witty commentary and expert opinions on the cultural sides of Web development, design and new technology, and Kottke succeeds in combining his discussion of Web news with a personal tone and the occasional personal story. The screenshot reproduced here (figure 4) shows an excellent example of this. When it was taken, Kottke and his wife (Meg Hourihan, who coincidentally was a co-founder of Blogger.com) had recently become parents for the first time. Kottke's blogging had therefore dropped to a minimum, but, when he did post, it was to compare his newborn son's reflexes to the motion-sensitivity of two recently released technological toys: the iPhone and the Wii game console's remote. After considering the various advantages and drawbacks of the iPhone and the Wiimote, he concludes that the baby is the winner:

> Newborns, however, are born with something called the <u>Moro reflex</u>. When infants feel themselves fall backwards, they startle and throw their arms out to the sides, as illustrated in <u>this video</u>. Even fast asleep they will do this, often waking up in the process. So while the Wiimote's accelerometer may be more sensitive, the psychological pressure exerted on the parent while lowering a sleeping baby slowly and smoothly enough so as not to wake them with the Moro reflex and thereby squandering 40 minutes of walking-the-baby-to-sleep time is beyond intense and so much greater than any stress one might feel serving for the match in tennis or getting that final strike in bowling.

In this cited portion, Kottke links out to information on newborn babies' 'accelerometer'; earlier in the post he has linked to information on the accelerometers built into the iPhone and the Wiimote. He does include a touch of a diary-style story about being a new parent, but its style is very different from Dooce's, woven into a discussion of recent technology.

Kottke's blog layout (see figure 4) shows his enthusiasm for and knowledge about the Web by integrating 'widgets', pieces of code that you can paste into your blog template to automatically display your activity on another site. Like most blogs, Kottke.org keeps the main content – the blog posts – in the widest column, and places extras (the title, the description, links and widgets) around the edges. When this screenshot was taken, Kottke had a widget at the top showing his most recent posts to Twitter.com, a site where people can exchange

Figure 4: A screenshot of Jason Kottke's blog, kottke.org (taken 2 August 2007).

short, SMS-length messages on the Web on their mobile phones.

Jason Kottke usually does not permit comments on his posts, presumably because of the extremely high number of comments he used to receive, making it very work-intensive to moderate comments and participate in discussions. However, readers have created a Web site of their own called *Kottke Komments*, which sucks in the posts from Kottke.org's RSS feed and republishes them, the main difference being that comments are open on each post. There are no links from Kottke.org to *Kottke Komments*, meaning it is hard for readers to find the site, and not many readers seem to participate in the discussions held there. Kottke does participate in conversations between blogs by linking to blogs in some of his posts, and he often acknowledges that he has found an interesting link or story in another blog by adding a line at the end of a post, for instance: 'via Matt', where the word Matt is linked to Matt's post at his blog *A Whole Lot of Nothing*. He doesn't have a blogroll, but includes a list of links to 'sites I've enjoyed recently' in the right-hand column of his blog, and there are several blogs among these.

Topic-driven Blogs: Dailykos.com

Jason Kottke and Heather Armstrong blog about issues that interest them. They don't limit their blogging to a pre-defined topic, although their interests are reasonably stable. Kottke is a graphic designer who mainly works with the Web, and so most of his posts are about the Web, design or information architecture. While Armstrong was in the tech industry she wrote about work and living in LA, whereas now her focus is largely on life as a mother of a small child. Despite changes in their lives, their individual voices are constant reminders that these blogs are personal.

Many blogs are not primarily focused on the varying interests of the individual blogger, but are instead focused on topics as diverse as knitting (*Brooklyn Tweed*), personal finances (*Get Rich Slowly*), fashion (*Style Bytes*), digital art and electronic literature (*GrandTextAuto*), politicians' use of the web (*techPresident*), quantum theory (*The Quantum Pontiff*) or personal productivity (*LifeHack*). All these topic-centred blogs share newly discovered ideas and information with their readers, usually providing links to more information. Thus they provide a filter to the vast amounts of news, information and conversations on the Web. While many of these blogs are run by individuals, topic-driven blogs are also often run collaboratively by a group of contributors. Often such blogs prioritize debate, both between posters and between posters and commentators.

There are as many different kinds of topic-driven blogs as there are hobbies, passions and professions. One large group within topic-driven blogs is blogs about politics. According to

Figure 5: A screenshot of the popular political weblog *Daily Kos* (dailykos.com), which is written by its founder Markos Moulitsas and a number of contributing editors. (Screenshot taken 2 August 2007)

Pew Internet Research's survey of bloggers in July 2006, around 11 per cent of all bloggers write primarily about politics. *Daily Kos*, a liberal blog founded by Markos Moulitsas in 2002, is one of the most popular political blogs. Moulitsas writes many of the posts himself, but also has a number of other contributors. In the screenshot shown in figure 5, the most recent post, which is the only post visible in the screenshot, was written by Mark Sumner, using the pseudonym Devilstower.

As you can see from figure 5, *Daily Kos* uses a similar layout to Kottke.org, except for two narrow side columns to the right instead of just one. The first side column contains ads, all political ads that agree with the blog's liberal point of view. There's another ad placed as a banner at the very top of the screen, above the title and cropped from the screenshot. This leads to a blog called *MotherTalkers*, so, while it's not a political ad like the others, it is an ad for a compatible product. And above the most recent post there's a little ad for a book published by *Daily Kos*. The second side column contains standard blog paratexts: links to other parts of the site, an 'about' section, and recommended posts, or diaries, as they call them on this site.

The post shown in the screenshot is titled 'The Fox News Candidate', and begins thus:

> If you were running for the Republican presidential nomination, whose support would be worth the equivalent of many millions in campaign dollars? Newt? Nah. Bush? Ha. Try Roger Ailes, <u>the head of Fox News</u> and former media adviser to Richard Nixon.

The post then continues with a couple of fairly extensive quotes and some further discussion. Even without reading the post you can see from its layout that quotations make up most of the text. This is the case in most posts on *Daily Kos* and on other political blogs. Posts tend to take a news article, a press release or another blog post as a starting point, show readers specific sections of the post, and criticize or add to the points made in the quotation. The posts link back to the source, allowing readers to read the entire article if they so wish. This form of blogging is discussion-oriented and can lead to extensive conversations across blogs. It is not at all confined to political blogs, but may be most prolific in these blogs.

Defining Blogs

The word blog is a contraction of the words Web and log. Blogs have developed considerably since the word was first used about a Web site in 1997, but the basic sense of a blog being some kind of log, kept on the Web, remains. The word log is taken from nautical navigation, and originally referred to a chronological record of events during a sea journey:

tracking speed, weather, course and so on. The name originally comes from the practice of measuring speed by throwing a log attached to a rope overboard and counting how many knots in the rope passed through a sailor's hands in thirty seconds. Readings from the log would then be entered into the logbook. Today, other information is also entered into the logbook. Weblogs have retained the chronological organization of the ship's logbook, although their content is less ordered and less systematic than the conventional logbook. The implicit transfer of the navigation metaphor to the Web is fitting, as people in the nineties tended to talk about navigating the Web.

The three examples we've looked at so far, *Dooce*, *Kottke* and *Daily Kos*, have many things in common. Their basic layout is similar, with the page divided into two or three columns, where the largest column is for the main content, the posts, and the narrower columns are kept for links to other blogs, information about the blog or blogger, links within the blog and ads. Two of the blogs are written by individuals and have very subjective, personal writing styles, whereas *Daily Kos* is written by a group of contributors and has a more journalistic style, although posts are clearly opinionated and don't attempt to be neutral or objective.

There are blogs about acrobatics, cars, fashion, fatherhood, finances, gadgets, gardening, happiness, health, knitting, life, mathematics, motherhood, movies, pets, philosophy, photography, poetry, politics, personal productivity, religion, technology, travel, writing, and, of course, blogging. If you're interested in any particular topic, you can probably find a blog – or a dozen blogs – about it. If not, you can easily start your own blog. But what do these very diverse Web sites have in common that allows us to call them all 'blogs'?

Genres may be defined by their form or by their content. Comedies, for instance, are largely defined by their content and theme. M. H. Abrams's *A Glossary of Literary Terms* (Abrams 1993) defines a comedy as 'a work in which the materials are selected and managed primarily in order to inter-est, involve, and amuse us: the characters and their discom-fitures engage our pleasurable attention rather than our profound concern, we are made to feel confident that no great disaster will occur, and usually the action turns out happily for the chief characters'. The sonnet, on the other hand, is an example of a genre that is defined by form alone. Abrams' defi-nition reads thus: 'Sonnet. A lyric poem consisting of a single *stanza* of fourteen iambic pentameter lines linked by an intri-cate rhyme scheme.' There is, admittedly, later in the defini-tion a discussion of the kinds of subject a sonnet typically addresses (sexual love was most common prior to John Donne, who introduced religious themes), but it is clear that the main defining quality of a sonnet is that it is constrained formally.

Blogs are far more diverse in their subject matter than either comedies or sonnets. On the other hand, blogs are easy to define formally, and, as we saw from looking at *Dooce, Kottke* and *Daily Kos*, blogs share similarities in layout and contain many of the same elements. The most obvious is the basic unit of the post, but there are many others, such as the timestamps, the post titles, the blogroll, the 'about' page and so on. Most def-initions of blogs rely primarily on the formal qualities of blogs. The Wikipedia entry for 'blog' begins, as of 28 August 2007, by stating that a blog is 'a Web site where entries are written in chronological order and commonly displayed in reverse chronological order'. This entry was begun on 1 November 2001, and has since been edited by hundreds of Wikipedia users, and thus we might assume that it represents a consen-sus opinion. The definition of 'weblog' that I wrote for the *Routledge Encyclopedia of Narrative Theory* begins in a similar manner, by stating that a weblog is 'a frequently updated Web site consisting of dated entries arranged in reverse chronologi-cal order so the most recent post appears first' (Walker 2005).

These can be taken as minimal definitions of a blog – how-ever, they are also so broad that they could include many forms of Web site that are not typically called blogs – company newsletters, for instance, or online newspapers. If we see blogs not as a genre but as a medium, that need not be a problem.

The difference between a medium and a genre has become blurred with the Internet. It's easy enough to say that television is a medium, and that soap operas, talk shows and sitcoms are genres. This differentiation is more difficult – and perhaps less useful – on the Internet. Scholars have suggested that, rather than looking at the Internet as a single medium, it makes more sense to consider different authoring software as providing different media (Ryan 2005). A game made in Flash is thus using a different medium, with different constraints and affordances, from a video edited in iMovie and uploaded to YouTube. In this sense of the word, blogs are a medium, not a genre. Just as an artist chooses to use oil paints rather than watercolour or a director chooses to work with cinema rather than television or theatre, a blogger has chosen to work within the set of constraints and affordances offered by blogging software.

Within the medium of blogs, you might then identify different genres and sub-genres, such as the diary-style blog, the filter blog or the political blog. Each of these carries a set of elective limitations – for instance, the filter blog would probably not include photographs on the blogger's cat, and the personal blog would probably not include frequent links to newspaper articles about politics or allow several posters. Of course, many blogs do cross genres, and as with every genre there are exceptions and crossovers.

Ultimately, whether or not you decide to define blogs as a medium or as a genre depends on your perspective. As Marie-Laure Ryan writes in her discussion of media and narrative for the *Routledge Encyclopedia of Narrative Theory*, the same thing might be seen as either a genre or a medium: 'Hypertext, for instance, is a genre if we view it as a type of text, but it is a (sub)medium if we regard it as an electronic tool for the organization of text' (Ryan 2005). We could say exactly the same thing of blogs. If we see blogs as a medium, then the formal definitions are sufficient. These are the material limitations of blogs. An online newspaper or company newsletter may well choose to use blogging software as a medium. However, if we see blogs as a genre, or, as Ryan puts it, as a 'type of text', then our definition should include mention of the typical style and content that lets us at a glance say 'that's not a blog' when we see an online newspaper.

The personal tone that we saw in Kottke's and Dooce's blogs is one of the characteristics often said to define blogs. Evan Williams, who, with Meg Hourihan, co-founded the company that created Blogger.com, names three characteristics that, to him, define blogging: frequency, brevity and personality (Turnball 2001). This triad refers to the familiar though not uncontroversial rules for good writing: clarity, brevity and sincerity, a triad Richard Lanham calls a 'venerable Stoic theory of language' (Lanham 1993, 228). Lanham argues that such rules for good writing belong to a world that revolves around goods and commodities, where words are derivative, simple references to the objects they refer to. In today's information society, on the other hand, 'words *are* the "goods"' (229), and striving to be 'clear, brief and sincere' makes no sense.

Be that as it may, William's alternative, 'frequency, brevity and personality', does describe the gist of blogging. The first two points describe formal qualities: blogs consist of frequent, relatively brief postings. The third is a question of style and context: blogs are personal. They are usually written by individuals, and present an individual's subjective view of – or log of – the Web, their life or a particular topic. Even company blogs tend to be written by an individual or a small group of individuals, as we will see in chapter 6. Blogs are generally written in the first person.

In addition to being a first person form of writing, blogs are social. Most blogs allow and encourage readers to leave comments, and almost all use links to link to sources and to other bloggers discussing similar topics. The social aspect of blogs is included in this definition of 'weblog' from the Oxford English Dictionary:

> A frequently updated Web site consisting of personal observations, excerpts from other sources, etc., typically run by a single person, and usually with hyperlinks to other sites; an online journal or diary.

It's probably not possible to construct a water-tight definition of 'blog' that once and for all enables us to classify any Web site as being either a blog or not a blog, but in most cases people have no trouble making such a distinction. One sure sign that a set of conventions for a genre has been established is the existence of parodies of the genre – and there are already many parodies of blogs. One of the most well known is *The Dullest Blog in the World*, an anonymous blog with very short, very dull entries. The last entry to be posted to the blog, 'Tidying Some Pencils', on 16 March 2006, gives a good impression of the style: 'Some pencils were scattered around on my desk. I picked them up one by one. I placed the pencils in the drawer which I use to store pencils.' Beneath each post are the standard auto-generated list of links to the comments on the post, a permalink (permanent link) to the post, and, of course, the date and time stamp. The most remarkable thing about *The Dullest Blog in the World* is the sheer volume of comments each post attracts. Many posts have hundreds of comments, showing how fascinated people are with this simple parody.

A Brief History of Weblogs

Weblogs are unequivocally a product of the Web, and their history can be said to have begun at the same time as the Web was born. The World Wide Web was invented by Tim Berners-Lee and first implemented at the end of 1990, when Berners-Lee finished building the tools necessary to publish and view the first Web site: a Web server on which to host the Web site, a

Web browser with which to view it, and the site itself. At the time, Berners-Lee was a scientist at CERN, the well-known particle physics lab in Switzerland, and his project was not seen as particularly important. The Internet had already existed for two decades, and was used by scientists, programmers and people interested in new forms of communication. Before the Web, the Internet ran a number of protocols, such as email, UseNet (discussion groups), IRC (a chat system) and Gopher (a way of browsing files on remote servers). Many people simply saw the World Wide Web as yet another protocol. Berners-Lee's prototype had a browser that was entirely text-based, so Web pages couldn't include images or other media as they do today, and the browsers were not available on most computer platforms. It wasn't until 1993 that the Web opened up to the general public with the release of Mosaic, the first widely available graphical Web browser, and also the first Web browser to allow embedded images. Previous browsers had displayed images in separate windows, not in the same window as the text.

While today's blogs are expected to change regularly – indeed, their chief defining feature is that they are frequently updated and that the content does not stay the same – most early Web sites were imagined as stable products. In retrospect, personal home pages can be seen as a precursor to blogs, but they were envisioned as complete presentations of the user's interests, not as something that would change daily. Web sites were, however, often published before their creators imagined them to be complete. 'Under construction' signs were a common sight on Web sites in the 1990s, often accompanied by an icon depicting a worker with a shovel, as on road signs.

By 1994, some pioneers had started online diaries. Justin Hall was one of the first diarists, but if you look at the early pages on his Web site you'll see that his site was very different from today's blogs. His Web site, links.net, is a wonderful example of the shift from building ever-expanding, densely hypertextual Web sites to developing blogs that are not intended to ever be completed. Hall used the section of his site called Vita to tell the story of his life. Some pages show links organized chronologically from his childhood to the present; others are organized thematically by family, the places he grew up in, places he travelled to, school, and people who meant a lot to him. Once you click a link you find yourself in a labyrinth of interlinked stories that keep leading you through parts of Hall's life, frequently circling back to certain key topics, such as his father's suicide when he was eight, or his fascination with the Web. In 1996, Hall began publishing diary entries (in a section of the site called Daze), but each entry still had the same rambling style as his autobiography. Hall didn't start using blogging software until 2003. Up until then, he hand-coded each entry.

When Justin Hall began publishing regular diary entries at links.net, his site matched today's understanding of what a blog might be. However, at the time, the word weblog didn't exist – or rather, the word existed, but was used for a different purpose. The term weblog was used in the early 1990s to refer to the log of visitors that a person who administers a Web server can see. A weblog showed the number of total hits a site had received, how many unique users had visited, how much data had been transferred and other information about the traffic to the site.

In December 1997, Jorn Barger proposed the term should be used differently (Blood 2000). Barger's new site, *Robot Wisdom*, was (and still is) a frequently updated list of links to other Web sites Barger has visited and wants to recommend, and Barger used the word weblog as part of the title of his site: *Robot Wisdom: A weblog by Jorn Barger*. This, it seems, was the first usage of the word weblog in this sense. *Robot Wisdom* was a very bare list of links, with little or no commentary to each link. This style is similar to the typical style of the more widely read *Scripting News* in the early years. *Scripting News* is the weblog of Dave Winer and was launched in April 1997, several months before *Robot Wisdom*, and also consisted of links to Web sites the blogger had seen with very minimal commentary. Here are the first few lines of Winer's very first post, with the links underlined:

> Tuesday, April 01, 1997
> Linkbot, Big Brother.
> Barry Frankel says Web Ads are Intrusive and Wesley Felter replies.
> Check this out. Amazing!
> MacWEEK: Goodbye AppleLink. (A tear comes to my eye . . .)

Compare this with a post by Josh Catone at *Read/Write Web* on 7 August 2007. *Read/Write Web* was one of the top ten most popular blogs at the time of this post, according to Technorati.com, and Catone is a blogger who often writes on topics similar to those of Winer.

> Online Ad Sales Growing, But Not At 'Premium' Sites
> According to an article in the Financial Times today, online ads are expected to outsell those in print newspapers in the US by 2011. A study by Veronis Suhler Stevenson (VSS), FT reports, predicts ad spending online will grow to $62 billion over the next three years, compared to $60 billion for newspapers.

The post then continues for more than 500 words, providing several links to articles and Web sites that give different perspectives on the issue – a recent *New York Times* article reporting that premium Web publishers have seen a slowing in ad sales, and an article that compares the drop to the dot com boom and subsequent crash in the late 1990s. Catone also provides original analysis, suggesting that the text ads bloggers often use, provided by Google's Adsense program, might be where the money is in this business. (See chapter 6 for more on advertising in blogs.)

The most obvious difference between Catone's 2007 post and Winer's 1997 post is that Catone's is far more verbose. It uses links to build an argument, providing considerable context and original ideas. Winer's 1997 posts are much closer to *Robot Wisdom*'s simple list of links, logging the Web sites visited in much the same manner as the history menu on your Web browser.

In part, this would seem to be a historical development from weblogs as sparse, minimal lists of links to weblogs as sites where writers pull ideas together from different Web sites and weave links into miniature essays. But in fact, both kinds of blog post have existed in parallel. An early blogger who wrote considerably more essayistic posts than Jorn Barger and Dave Winer is Peter Merholz, who was the first person to shorten the term 'weblog' to 'blog'. Merholz simply noted this in the sidebar to his blog in 1999: 'I've decided to pronounce the word "weblog" as wee'- blog. Or "blog" for short' (Blood 2000). Merholz's posts to his blog *PeterMe* have consistently been more essayistic than sparse.

Early bloggers hand-coded their sites, meaning that they had to create their blogs from scratch and edit raw HTML code, or use a visual HTML editor like Dreamweaver, each time they updated the blog. In late 1998 and throughout 1999, several free tools appeared that allowed bloggers to easily publish and update blogs and online diaries using templates and Web-based forms where posts could simply be typed straight in. Open Diary launched in October 1998, offering online diarists free hosting and an easy publishing solution. By January 1999, it hosted 2500 diaries, all of them anonymous. In fact, Open Diary required that users be anonymous:

> The Open Diary is a totally anonymous diary community. We don't want to know who you are, and we don't want your readers to know who you are. Therefore, please do not include any information in your diary that would identify you. Such information includes full names, street addresses, phone numbers, and e-mail addresses that include your name in them (like JohnSmith@xyz.com).
>
> We do not allow any such information on this site, and if you enter it, it will be deleted. [. . .] Remember, there is a potential

audience of 100 million people on the Internet who could read
your diary, we would prefer (and we think you would also) if
they didn't know who you are. (opendiary.com, 'The Rules',
accessed at thearchive.org's archive for 25 January 1999)

Early weblogs differed from many online diaries in that they
were generally written by people who used their full name,
and, of course, in that they primarily consisted of comments
on other Web sites and not of diary-like discussions of the
writer's own life.

1999 also saw the launch of Pitas, the first free weblogging
tool, followed by the release of Blogger in August of the same
year. In her early essay on weblogs, Rebecca Blood argued that
the actual posting interface of Blogger may have influenced the
way weblogs developed in this period, from being sparse lists
of links, like Barger and Winer's early posts, to being more
essayistic, including thoughts on issues not directly related to
a specific Web site, and links to other blogs that led to conversations between blogs (Blood 2000). When you posted to your
Blogger blog in 1999, the interface looked quite similar to the
2007 interface shown in figure 2, with a small box for you to
type the post's title, and a larger box for you to type whatever
you like. Other blogging systems, like that at the still popular
community blog *Metafilter*, had and still have a more rigid
system. At *Metafilter*, you fill out several boxes, each clearly
labelled with instructions to the writer:

- Post Title. Keep it short and descriptive.
- Link URL. Web address of the site you're posting about.
- Link Text. These will be the first words of your post, and will
  be a clickable link to the Web address you entered above.
- Description. The body of your post. Feel free to add links
  within your description, keep it one paragraph long if possible, line breaks will be stripped.

This leads to a very specific form of post that is quite similar to
the early style of Winer and Barger. For instance, in August
2007, one could read posts such as the following:

The Icelandic coastline. A gallery of photos of the rugged, cold, and beautiful coast of Iceland.

posted by Gamblor at 5:40 AM – 18 comments

Time lapse animations of planets and satellites. See what an amateur digital astrophotographer could do a decade ago. This is what the animated gif was designed to do.

posted by dkg at 6:43 AM – 20 comments

Statetris is Tetris with European countries or American states as blocks.

posted by goodnewsfortheinsane at 8:53 PM – 27 comments

As you can see, the posts match the constraints set up by the four boxes of *Metafilter*'s posting interface. There are exceptions, as it is possible to compose a post without using the initial link, but *Metafilter* is heavily dominated by brief, sparse posts linking to one or more interesting or unusual Web sites. The comments, however, can develop into lengthy debates, often involving scores and sometimes hundreds of participants.

By the year 2000, Rebecca Blood wrote that the transition from the sparse lists of links, or filter-style weblogs, as she calls them, to the more essayistic form of blogging had largely taken place. She credits the free-form interface of blogging sites like Blogger with this shift:

> It is this free-form interface combined with absolute ease of use which has, in my opinion, done more to impel the shift from the filter-style weblog to journal-style blog than any other factor. And there has been a shift. Searching for a filter-style weblog by clicking through the thousands of weblogs listed at weblogs.com, the EatonWeb Portal, or Blogger Directory can be a Sisyphean task. (Blood 2000)

Another factor in the shift is likely to be the merging of genres. Early Web diaries such as that of Justin Hall have little in common with the early weblogs of Jorn Barger or Dave Winer, or with the *Metafilter* of today. Carolyn Burke, who started her online diary in January 1995, wrote at The Online Diary History Project, 'I wanted everyone in the world to expose their inner lives to everyone else. Complete open honest people. What a great and ideal world would result' (Burke, not dated). There was certainly a heavy dose of utopianism and optimism going around. Blogger's slogan in 2000, 'Push-button publishing for the people', takes another tack on the matter – not shared intimacy, but opening up publishing to regular people.

Once blogging systems like Blogger.com and others were established, blogging took off. By 2002, the *Oxford English Dictionary* was asking Peter Merholz for a print source for the word 'blog', so they could include it in their dictionary (peterme.com, 14 June 2002).

The blog search engine Technorati.com launched in 2003. The number of blogs it tracked grew rapidly, from a little over 100,000 in late 2003 to three million by July 2004. At this point, the total number of blogs was doubling every few months. That year, the Merriam-Webster declared 'blog' to be the word of the year, reporting that 'blog' was the most searched-for word on their online dictionary that year. By then, the media were writing about blogs regularly and almost everybody seemed to have heard about them. But in a survey late that year, 62 per cent of Internet users still said they didn't know what a blog was (Rainie 2005). No wonder they were trying to look the word up in a dictionary.

It's impossible to know exactly how many blogs there are. One problem is the number of inactive blogs. Many people will try to create a blog to see how it works, but then abandon the blog after a single post, or maybe after a week or two. The reverse problem occurs with spam blogs, blogs created by marketers and spammers that are simply foils for search engines, full of garbled, machine-generated posts that link to Web sites that the spammers want search engines to see as popular. Another reason why it's hard to track blogs accurately is that the Internet is distributed and there is no central counting house for blogs.

By 2007, the pace of growth had slowed somewhat, but was still steady. Technorati tracked over 70 million weblogs in April 2007 (Sifry 2007).

Rebecca Blood wrote in 2000:

> The promise of the Web was that everyone could publish, that a thousand voices could flourish, communicate, connect. The truth was that only those people who knew how to code a Web page could make their voices heard. Blogger, Pitas, and all the rest have given people with little or no knowledge of HTML the ability to publish on the Web: to pontificate, remember, dream, and argue in public, as easily as they send an instant message. (Blood 2000)

To judge by the success of blogging in the last few years, it seems that the 'push-button publishing' Blogger.com offered in October 2000 was exactly what the people wanted.

CHAPTER TWO

From Bards to Blogs

Blogs are part of a fundamental shift in how we communicate. Just a few decades ago, our media culture was dominated by a small number of media producers who distributed their publications and broadcasts to large, relatively passive audiences. Today, newspapers and television stations have to adapt to a new reality, where ordinary people create media and share their creations online. We have moved from a culture dominated by mass media, using one-to-many communication, to one where participatory media, using many-to-many communication, is becoming the norm.

Blogs tend to be understood in terms of their differences in comparison to the mass media that dominated the twentieth century. This is especially true in the media's presentation of blogs, which repeatedly attempts to understand blogs as a (possibly flawed) form of journalism. Journalism is a profession with conventions that have evolved alongside the technology of mass publication and mass broadcasting and that are contingent both on this technology and on the commercial aspects of selling newspapers and broadcast media to both consumers and to advertisers. We'll return to the question of blogs and journalism in chapter 4.

If we step back a little further, and look at the larger picture of communication and publication through the ages, blogs make more sense than if we see them strictly from the point of view of mass media. Rather than simply being a form born in opposition to mass media, blogs have aspects in common with many other forms of communication during the last centuries.

The mass media are not a very old phenomenon. Before the introduction of print, mass distribution was impossible. True, kings might hire scores of scribes to write out their instructions in many copies to be spread throughout the kingdom, but most books and written materials only existed in a limited number of copies. If you wanted to read a particular book, you would have to travel to the monastery or nobleman's library in which it was kept, and ask for permission to read it. As print became commonplace throughout the sixteenth century and onwards, a great shift occurred in our understanding of what literature and information was. When we learnt to record and broadcast sound and, later, moving images, sounds and images became governed by the same logic of distribution and ownership as print had been.

This chapter traces the history of communication and publication as it relates to blogs. The histories of technological innovations such as writing, print and the Web are intertwined with philosophical understandings of the importance of communication, such as Plato's resistance to the written word, the different values assigned to dissemination and dialogue, ideas of the public sphere and, in our own century, the visionary ideas of how computers might change our culture. Towards the end of the chapter, we'll discuss how these cultural and technological aspects can be thought of as influencing each other, either by seeing one as leading the way or by seeing them as mutual participants in a process of co-construction.

Orality and Literacy

There were at least two major shifts in communication prior to the advent of broadcast media and, more recently, the Internet. The introduction of print and the subsequent ability to mass produce identical copies of a work was one, but prior to that came the introduction of writing itself. We often forget that writing is a technology in itself, even without the printing press or the computer. When writing was first introduced, it was met both with excitement and with a great deal of scepticism.

Looking back to the transition from orality to literacy – from a purely oral culture to one in which writing played an important part – can be useful in understanding the cultural meaning of blogging. Our transition from print to electronic media has been characterized by the scholar Walter Ong as a *secondary orality*, a return in some ways to a culture more like that of the Ancient Greeks than of the post-Gutenberg society (Ong 1982). By electronic media, Ong meant radio and television, not the Internet, writing as he was before the Internet was generally available to the public. Some aspects of blogging are certainly very similar to oral cultures: blogs are conversational and social, they are constantly changing and their tone tends to be less formal and closer to everyday speech than is the general tone of print writing.

Plato's dialogues deal with precisely the transition from speech to writing as the privileged form of discourse. His dialogues are written renditions of oral conversations between Socrates and various students, and so the arguments Plato makes are presented as belonging to Socrates, Plato's teacher. The dialogue *Phaedrus* takes writing itself as its main topic. You may have heard of one of Plato's objections to writing: it will destroy memory. People won't bother to memorize facts, speeches or stories if they can easily access them in writing. Another objection Plato makes to writing is far more relevant to blogging. Plato complains that a written text is basically unresponsive. If you ask a person what he means by what he just said, he will answer you. If you try to ask a text a question, however, it will 'preserve a solemn silence' (Plato 1999) and cannot defend itself. Even if a text is proven to be false, the words will stay the same, while a living person might not continue to make the same false claim.

With the Internet, this is no longer true of writing. Blogs can be and frequently are edited, with corrections being made after a post's initial publication. Most blogs allow comments, which means that you *can* ask a question of these texts, and, quite probably, the text will respond – or rather its writer, the blogger, will answer your question. If the blogger herself does not answer, other readers are likely to do so, either in the comments to the blog itself, or in their own blogs. In this sense, blogs appear to be closer to the reciprocity of oral communication that Plato appreciates than to the unresponsiveness of writing. Perhaps, then, blogs are part of the secondary orality that Walter Ong wrote of.

Another issue Plato raises with respect to writing is the way in which writing allows words to be distributed where or when the writer is not present. Words should not be cast out indiscriminately, Plato argues, they should be like seeds planted carefully in a mind that is ready for them, and they should be nurtured through conversation, in dialogue. Spreading words indiscriminately is wasteful, and a serious scholar would not do so: 'Then he will not seriously incline to "write" his thoughts "in water" with pen and ink, sowing words which can neither speak for themselves nor teach the truth adequately to others' (Plato 1999). Plato himself writes, of course, rendering his argument ambiguous at best, but his point is valid. Up until medieval times, courts of law held witnesses to be more reliable than documents such as contracts, thinking witnesses 'more credible than texts because they could be challenged and made to defend their statements, which texts could not' (Ong 1982, 96).

Plato wrote dialogues, and he praises dialogue as a form of communication that is more valuable than dissemination, such as writing or a public speech given to a large audience. In much writing on new media and the Internet, the dialogic nature of the Web is similarly lauded. However, in his history of communication, John Durham Peters seeks to dispel the 'often uncritical celebration of dialogue', writing that '[d]ialogue is only one communicative script among many. The lament over the end of conversation and the call for refreshed dialogue alike miss the virtues inherent in nonreciprocal forms of action and culture' (Peters 1999, 35).

Peters sees Plato and Jesus as Western culture's primordial spokesmen for dialogue and dissemination respectively. While Plato argues in the *Phaedrus* that one who would share his ideas should do so in person and in a close dialogue, Jesus told the Parable of the Sower, who spread his seed indiscriminately, spreading out a message to the masses:

> A farmer went out to sow his seed. As he was scattering the seed, some fell along the path, and the birds came and ate it up. Some fell on rocky places, where it did not have much soil. It sprang up quickly, because the soil was shallow. But when the sun came up, the plants were scorched, and they withered because they had no root. Other seed fell among thorns, which grew up and choked the plants. Still other seed fell on good soil, where it produced a crop – a hundred, sixty or thirty times what was sown. He who has ears, let him hear. (Matthew 13: 3–9)

As Peters points out, Plato argues for the exact opposite strategy, mocking the careless farmer who plants his seeds in unfitting soil:

> Would a husbandman, who is a man of sense, take the seeds, which he values and which he wishes to bear fruit, and in sober seriousness plant them during the heat of summer, in some garden of Adonis, that he may rejoice when he sees them in eight days appearing in beauty? At least he would do so, if at all, only for the sake of amusement and pastime. But when he is in earnest he sows in fitting soil, and practises husbandry, and is satisfied if in eight months the seeds which he has sown arrive at perfection. (Plato 1999)

Both these parables or stories are metaphors for the best way of sharing ideas. The Parable of the Sower proposes that you should spread your message as broadly as possible and accept that not everyone will understand or wish to engage with your ideas. This, Peters writes, is how *dissemination* works (note that the root of the word dissemination, *sem*, means seed). Even though many or maybe most seeds will be lost, the benefit will be great: 'But the one who received the seed that fell on good soil is the man who hears the word and understands it. He produces a crop, yielding a hundred, sixty or thirty times what was sown' (Matthew 13: 23). Mass media clearly follows this model – a television broadcast will be watched by only a small proportion of the people who could potentially tune in to it, but that small proportion may be sufficient for the producers. Advertisers and telemarketers routinely try to spread their message to as many people as possible, and are often more than happy if 1 per cent or even fewer of the recipients take up their offer.

Plato, on the other hand, argues that dissemination is wasteful, and that dialogue with worthy listeners and the careful tending of communication is the best way to spread your ideas. This idealization of dialogue has been particularly strong in modern ideas of pedagogy, where experts in the latter half of the twentieth century have moved away from previous ideas of education as a simple transferral of information (a kind of dissemination) and towards the idea that knowledge is constructed by the learner in dialogue and interaction with people and technologies. Dialogue has also been hailed as one of the key features of new media, and especially of the Internet.

Blogs are remarkable for combining aspects of both dialogue and dissemination. In a sense, they are as promiscuously sown as the seeds in the Parable of the Sower. Blogs are published on the Internet and can be read by anybody – or nobody. On the other hand, a successful blog must be tended as a garden (Matrullo 2002). A reader can ask a question of a blog, by leaving a comment on the blog itself or by posting on her own blog, and very often the blogger will respond. Well-tended blogs are not at all like the writings of which Plato complains, 'if you ask them a question they preserve a solemn silence' (Plato 1999).

The Introduction of Print

'The print-made split between heart and head is the trauma that affects Europe from Machiavelli to the present', Marshall

McLuhan wrote in *The Gutenberg Galaxy* (1962, 170). McLuhan wrote in aphorisms offering outrageously vivid ideas, but, as Elizabeth Eisenstein, a later historian of the transition to print, has pointed out, a statement like that just quoted cannot be tested and is thus difficult to build upon (Eisenstein 1979, 129). Eisenstein and others have, however, detailed many aspects inherent in the transition from a society where spoken discourse was the norm to one where silent reading and writing was a main form of communication.

Eisenstein argues that the introduction of print was a major influence on the way Western culture developed from the fifteenth century onward. The printing press was first invented by the Chinese in the eleventh century, but was little used because of the enormous number of characters in the Chinese alphabet. Its European invention, which was apparently independent of the Chinese technology, is credited to Johannes Gutenberg around 1439. Previously, woodblock printing had been used; Gutenberg's important innovation was the use of movable type. By using individual letters, printers no longer had to carve out a whole page at a time, but could set type more flexibly and more easily make changes or corrections. Moveable type was quicker and the results were more durable. Print did not immediately change books, it took fifty or a hundred years for print to become a more or less standardized process.

Eisenstein numbers six features of print that caused changes in our culture:

1. Dissemination
2. Standardization
3. Reorganization
4. Data collection
5. Preservation
6. Amplification and Reinforcement

Perhaps the radical increase of *dissemination* was the most obvious feature of print. While manuscripts were rare and costly objects, print allowed many identical copies of a text to be made. Instead of scholars travelling to a text, texts were spread throughout the world on a scale never before seen. When Eisenstein describes the 'ferment engendered by access to more books' (Eisenstein 1979, 74), it is easy to see the parallels to the radical increase in access to texts that has become possible with the Web.

One advantage of increased dissemination was that bringing texts together showed contradictions between them. For instance, having three different atlases side by side, it would become very obvious if a country were portrayed differently in the different maps. This led to a greater level of *standardization*. Additionally, errors were dealt with in a more systematic manner. A scribe might make an error when he copied a single book. But with print, any error was replicated in all the copies, as with the 'wicked bible' of 1631, where the printers forgot the word 'not', thus making the seventh commandment read 'Thou shalt commit adultery.' The unfortunate printers were fined 300 pounds, a life-time's wages, and all but eleven copies of the book have since been destroyed. This kind of mistake led, among other things, to the publication of *errata*, lists of known errors, and, with that, to a willingness to try to find and minimize errors.

Print also led to the *reorganization* of texts, as new standards were developed. Tables of contents, indices and alphabetical organization were not common before print, and readers had to learn skills that today are taken for granted. For instance, Eisenstein quotes a 1604 edition of an English dictionary as noting at the beginning that 'the reader must learne the alphabet, to wit: the order of the letters as they stand' (Eisenstein 1979, 89). Today we teach toddlers their ABCs.

The increased number of readers also led to radical improvements in *data collection*, Eisenstein's fourth item. An example of this is Ortelius' great atlas project, the *Theatrum orbis terrarum*, first published in 1570. Ortelius requested amendments and corrections to the maps presented in his atlas. The *Theatrum* was frequently revised on the basis of feedback received from readers all around Europe, and was republished in at least twenty-eight editions before Ortelius' death in 1598. Eisenstein notes that this kind of large-scale conversation about a topic was simply not possible before print: 'After printing, large-scale data-collection [became] subject to new forms of feed-back which had not been possible in the age of scribes' (1979, 111).

Eisenstein's fifth point is *preservation*. Although we do still have some copies of medieval manuscripts, and even of a few older documents, handwriting does not last forever. If it is copied, there will almost always be some degree of textual drift, because copyists always make small mistakes. Of course, printed documents don't last forever either, but, because they exist in a great many more copies, the likelihood of some copies remaining and perhaps being reprinted is far greater.

Finally, Eisenstein argues that print augments the *amplification and reinforcement* of ideas. This particularly shows itself in print culture's use and re-use of particular passages from ancient texts. We have very limited access to these scribal sources, but with print, we tend to replicate the same parts again and again – for instance, Plato's arguments against writing, which you have probably heard before and which were replicated again just a few pages ago.

Print, Blogging and Reading

Another deep way in which print influenced our culture in general and communication in particular is the increase in literacy that occurred with the greater access to books. Today, new kinds of literacy are developing as the general population is acquiring new skills and the ability both to read and navigate the Web and to publish its own words, images, videos, blogs and other content. These new literacies have been called network literacy, multi-literacies, digital literacy and secondary literacy.

The spread of print went hand in hand with the spread of literacy, that is, with the ability to read and write. It's difficult to measure the level of literacy historically, because some people could read but not write, while others could sign their name on a contract but not write anything else. However, estimates suggest that, in most of Europe, only 20–30 per cent of the population were literate in the early seventeenth century, while 70–90 per cent were literate by end of eighteenth century (Chartier 2001, 125).

Up until the fifteenth century, reading generally meant reading aloud. Often a reader would read for an audience. Around this time, which you will have noticed also coincides with the introduction of print, more and more people were learning to read and they were learning to read *silently*. Silent reading, which we so take for granted today, had radical effects. With silent reading, reading changed from a communal to a personal act, and it has been argued that this new solitary relationship between an individual and a text was a significant reason for the development of the notion of a separation between private and public (Chartier 2001). The solitude of reading and writing is, perhaps, changing with blogs, which are more explicitly social forms of writing.

On the one hand, a movement away from speeches, which drew people together as they listened, to printed reports, which caused people to draw apart as they read, could be said to have led to major changes in community structures. On the other hand, the fact that people unknown to one another could now read the same text allowed for a new kind of impersonal connection between people. Today's niche communities online are in a sense a more fully evolved version of this.

Printed Precedents of Blogs

Print media have been dominated by mass publishing, by dissemination rather than dialogue, but print also allows small scale and personal print publication. In the seventeenth century, pamphlets were the radical new form of communication, popular and widespread due to the combination of the

printing press, higher literacy levels and the lifting of censorship. As a history of pamphlets published in 1715 states, a
pamphlet, being 'of a small portable bulk, and of no great
price, and of no great difficulty, seems adapted for every one's
understanding, for every one's reading, for every one's buying
capacity and ability' (Davies 1715, quoted by Knights 2005,
224–5). Periodicals also became popular during this period.
In Britain this was due, in part, to the lifting of government
censorship of publications in 1695 (Knights 2005, 225). Like
with blogging, the spread of polemical printed publications
led to more publication:

> [P]rint was a dialogic medium: published claim provoked
> printed counter-claim, vindication, denial, or agreement.
> Such a dialogue was easiest to sustain during periods of press
> freedom – either when the laws regulating the press had
> lapsed (1641, 1679, 1695) or when the law was ineffectually
> enforced. The dialogue was necessary because the best way to
> counteract print, it came to be recognized, was through print.
> The more controversial print there was, the more need there
> was to enter into print to engage with it. (Knights 2005, 235)

In the nineteenth century, authors we today know chiefly as
novelists also edited and published their own personal newspapers. Alexandre Dumas directed and/or wrote for eleven
newspapers – he was truly into the new technology of the
modern press, introduced in France in the 1830s. Dumas' first
newspaper was written solely by Dumas himself, and was
called *Le Mois*, with a tag line that sounds so bloggish it must
be in use by some blogger, somewhere: *jour par jour, heure par
heure* ('day by day, hour by hour'). Dumas' intention was to
write a daily chronicle of events.

   In the twentieth century, print publication outside of large
mass media institutions and advertising was aided by the
technology of photocopying. Newsletters for schools, fanzines
and photocopied annual family letters are all examples of
small-scale, amateur publication. Some blogs serve the exact
same purposes as these, and are primarily intended for

small-scale distribution, with little idea of the communication being two-way. Indeed, Michael Faris argues that 'zines, that is, amateur, independently produced magazines, are a direct ancestor of blogs (Faris 2007).

The greatest difference between a blog and a photocopied school newsletter, or an annual family letter photocopied and mailed to a hundred friends, is the potential audience and the increased potential for direct communication between audience members as well as via the central hub of the blog. Although most blogs are only read by a small group of people, some of the audience will be random. A blog may suddenly gain popularity by being linked from other sites. Photocopied newsletters or fanzines, on the other hand, can in theory be re-photocopied and occasionally become cult phenomena, but the process is far more labour-intensive and in most cases too slow to gather the momentum that causes fads to spread on the Web.

So, while, as Marshall McLuhan argued, 'print makes everyone a reader, and Xerox makes everyone a publisher' (McLuhan 1977, 178), photocopiers don't change authorship greatly. Bloggers, on the other hand, or at least savvy bloggers, are aware that their audience may be greater than they imagine, and they know that they cannot control who is reading. That presumably changes the way we write.

The Late Age of Print

We are living in the Late Age of Print, Jay David Bolter wrote nearly two decades ago (Bolter 1991). As we are nearing the end of the first decade of the twenty-first century, we may be well on our way out of the Age of Print, late or otherwise. Recently, Tom Pettitt referred to the cultural period roughly between the introduction of print and the introduction of the Web as the Gutenberg parenthesis (Pettitt 2007). Pettitt calls the period dominated by print culture a parenthesis to emphasize that the mindset connected to print is temporary and that, from a broad historical perspective, it only affected a relatively brief period.

Before the introduction of print, Pettitt argues, literature and art were seen as malleable, flexible and changing. A story would be performed again and again, told by a storyteller or enacted in a theatre. A song or a tune would have no owner, but be played in different ways by different people. With the introduction of print, we began to think of literature as something that could be fixed. A book became an autonomous unit, it became an original object that could belong to someone – an author or a publisher. This led, in time, to the Romantic idea of the author or artist as an original genius. Pettitt argues that different art forms entered the Gutenberg parenthesis at different points in time. Poetry, for instance, entered it early, with fixed versions of texts appearing as early as the fourteenth century, before print. Theatre was later, with Shakespeare a transitional figure. Shakespeare used other narratives freely, but, once a version of the play had been printed, it was seen as fixed, as an autonomous original. Blues music didn't enter the parenthesis until the 1950s, when the standards began to be recorded by specific artists, who thereafter 'owned' the song.

However, print still holds strong as the culturally most respected medium. Print is the dominant medium used in schools, and reading of print literature is the only consumption of media that is seen as so culturally important that governments fund programmes to increase its use in the general population. Organizations such as the National Endowment for the Arts in the United States publish reports mourning the decrease in the reading of print novels and poetry, citing these figures as symptoms of a general crisis, as in their 2004 report, 'Reading at Risk':

> [P]rint culture affords irreplaceable forms of focused attention and contemplation that make complex communications and insights possible. To lose such intellectual capability – and the many sorts of human continuity it allows – would constitute a vast cultural impoverishment. (National Endowment for the Arts 2004)

This is a common idea: that print privileges 'focused attention' against broadcast media's channel surfing and the Web's hypertextuality with its link-following connectivity. The opposite argument can also be made. In his popular book *Everything Bad is Good for You*, Steven Johnson (2005) puts forth the argument that video games and television are actually giving us 'cognitive workouts' that teach the same kinds of skills as maths and chess. Television narratives involve far more complex storylines today than thirty years ago, while video games require constant problem solving. It is also worth noting that the most recent medium, the Internet, is increasing the amount of reading and writing people engage in, a form of textual practice that is completely ignored by the 'Reading at Risk' report.

With every media shift there have been sceptical voices lamenting the loss of whatever characteristics the previously dominant medium was perceived as promoting. As discussed earlier in this chapter, Plato famously argued that writing has great disadvantages in comparison to oral dialogue.

Today the ascendancy of print is waning, and, while print is still privileged by schools and the National Endowment for the Arts, it is no longer the dominant cultural medium. In the second half of the twentieth century radio and television moved in upon print's territory. In 2004, statistics for the USA show Americans watching an average of over four hours of television every day, and additionally listening to two hours and forty-two minutes of radio. They only spend half an hour a day reading newspapers and about twenty minutes a day reading books (US Census Bureau 2006).

In the last couple of decades, the Internet and computers have become increasingly important, although the use of the Internet still lags behind television and radio use. In 2004, US residents spent about the same amount of time on the Internet as they did reading newspapers – roughly half an hour a day (US Census Bureau 2006, Table 1110). However, these averages hide large differences in Internet use between different groups of the population. Nearly three quarters of all 18 to 44 year olds accessed the Internet during a typical week, against only 27 per cent of those aged 65 and above. Gender makes little difference to access rates, but the highly educated are far more likely to have accessed the Internet in the last week, as are those with high household incomes (Table 1112). And while over 90 per cent of households have televisions, only 54 per cent of households have access to the Internet from home. On the other hand, the percentage of the population to have watched television in the last week is stable across different demographics. The consumption of print is stable across age groups, but increases with higher levels of education and income.

While use of the Internet is clearly increasing, this does not seem to be at the cost of other media usage, which remains stable. It seems likely that some media are used simultaneously – people might surf the Internet while watching television, for instance, or read the newspaper while the radio is on in the background.

There are fairly large differences between Internet usage in different countries. Only 54 per cent of US households have Internet access, but in Norway the figure is considerably higher, at 79 per cent. While Norwegians watch less television than Americans (two and a half hours a day), the relationships between Internet usage and television viewing appear to be similar: television viewing remains stable, while Internet usage is increasing (Statistics Norway 2007).

A 2006 survey of the UK, France, Germany, Italy and Spain shows that most Europeans still use the Internet less than Americans do, but that time spent on the Internet now surpasses that spent with newspapers and journals (Edgecliffe-Johnson 2006). In the UK, about 60 per cent of the population is online on any day, against 82 per cent that watches television daily, according to National Statistics Online. There is no data for the amount of time spent online or watching television.

A Modern Public Sphere?

The public sphere is a concept introduced by Jürgen Habermas to describe an ideal democratic space for rational debate among informed and engaged citizens, a space that would thus be an arena mediating between state and society (Habermas 1991). While the idea that such a public sphere has ever existed has often been criticized, the concept is as frequently invoked, and many scholars have discussed its relevance to the Web and to blogging (Poster 1997; Baoill 2004; Notaro 2006; Boeder 2005; Bahnisch 2006).

Habermas connects the establishment of a modern conception of private and public to the establishment of a liberal, capitalist society, where news became a commodity sold by merchants. This led to the eighteenth- and nineteenth-century cultures of open debate in newspapers and in the coffee shops of large European cities. The open debates that occur in such a public sphere are seen as necessary to a true democracy.

The decline of the public sphere has regularly been lamented. Richard Sennett (1986) ties the decline to electronic media, though, writing before the Web, he refers primarily to radio and television. To Sennett, the one-way, mass broadcasting of radio and television made reasoning and debate between individuals almost impossible: 'Electronic communications is one means by which the very idea of public life has been put to an end. The media have vastly increased the store of knowledge social groups have about each other, but have rendered actual contact unnecessary' (282).

Sennett admits that this is not solely the fault of electronic media, writing that they merely fulfil 'those cultural impulses that formed over the whole of the last century and a half to withdraw from social interaction in order to know and feel more as a person' (282–3). He sees this tendency as having begun in nineteenth-century theatres and concert halls, where a 'crowd silence' (283) was for the first time established as a norm. Electronic media, Sennett argues, intensify this: 'You've got to be silent to be spoken to . . . Passivity is the "logic" of this technology' (283).

Today, audiences are anything but passive. According to a 2005 survey reported in the Norwegian newspaper *Dagbladet* (17 October 2005), in an average week every third Norwegian published something online. A more recent survey found that 38 per cent of Norwegians have appeared on television, showing that the increased participation in media is not limited to the Internet (*Forskning.no*, 22 September 2006). Mainstream media publications pander to our eagerness to share our views. Newspapers have expanded the traditional letters to the editor columns to allow readers to comment on individual articles in their online editions, and often provide an infrastructure for online discussion boards and blogging. The *New York Times* and several other online newspapers show ranked lists of the articles that readers have most frequently read, emailed and blogged. In television, phoning in has expanded into SMS TV, where talk shows, quiz shows and music shows all encourage viewers to send in SMSs that are either displayed on the screen for all viewers to see or function as votes: which politician do you agree with? what's the answer to the quiz? which team member shall we vote out of the Big Brother house? which music video shall we play next?

As we saw, Plato distrusted the indiscriminate spread of words. Jürgen Habermas recently expressed a similar concern about the Internet:

> On the one hand, the communication shift from books and the printed press to the television and the Internet has brought about an unimagined broadening of the media sphere, and an unprecedented consolidation of communication networks. Intellectuals used to swim around in the public sphere like fish in water, but this environment has become ever more inclusive, while the exchange of ideas has become more intensive than ever. But on the other hand the intellectuals seem to be suffocating from the excess of this vitalising element, as if they were overdosing. The blessing seems to have become a curse. I see the reasons for

that in the de-formalisation of the public sphere, and in the de-differentiation of the respective roles.

Use of the Internet has both broadened and fragmented the contexts of communication. This is why the Internet can have a subversive effect on intellectual life in authoritarian regimes. But at the same time, the less formal, horizontal cross-linking of communication channels weakens the achievements of traditional media. This focuses the attention of an anonymous and dispersed public on select topics and information, allowing citizens to concentrate on the same critically filtered issues and journalistic pieces at any given time. The price we pay for the growth in egalitarianism offered by the Internet is the decentralised access to unedited stories. In this medium, contributions by intellectuals lose their power to create a focus. (Habermas 2006)

If we read blogs through the eyes of Plato and Habermas, it seems that the authority of blogs might not to be tied simply to who can write them (anyone) but also to who can read them. If we have too many writers and readers, we might, to use Habermas' words, suffocate 'from the excess of this vitalising element'. In seventeenth- and eighteenth-century Britain, similar criticisms were made of the coffee houses Habermas lauded as the birthing place of the public sphere: 'the common people talke anything, for every carman and porter is now a statesman; and indeed the coffee houses are good for nothing else' (Sir Thomas Piper, quoted in Knights 2005, 251). Broad dissemination clearly worries many. Free dissemination means a lack of authority, and, ultimately, a lack of control.

Hypertext and Computer Lib

Hypertext, which blogs depend upon, is considerably older than the World Wide Web. The idea of hypertext is usually traced back to Vannevar Bush, science advisor to President Roosevelt during the Second World War. After the war was over, Bush wrote an influential essay titled 'As We May Think' (1945), which was published in the widely read journal *Atlantic*

Monthly. In this article, Bush argued that science had helped humanity to advance in many fields, including medicine, construction and even warfare. However, science had not yet been used to help us *think* more efficiently. In particular, Bush noted the difficulty of accessing new information effectively. The problem, he wrote, was 'not so much that we publish unduly in view of the extent and variety of present day interests, but rather that publication has been extended far beyond our present ability to make real use of the record'. Bush therefore proposed a new device that would help us store and access publications, and named this imagined device the memex:

> Consider a future device for individual use, which is a sort of mechanized private file and library. It needs a name, and, to coin one at random, 'memex' will do. A memex is a device in which an individual stores all his books, records, and communications, and which is mechanized so that it may be consulted with exceeding speed and flexibility. It is an enlarged intimate supplement to his memory.

Bush sketched a design for the memex that proposed having microfilm copies of books and other records built into a desk that would allow the reader to access two screens, each of which would project a page of a document. The controls on the desk would allow readers to make connections, or links, between documents, and to add notes. Bush even imagined a profession of 'trail-blazers', people who built trails of links through documents. If you were interested in a particular topic, you could then not only purchase a book about the topic, you could purchase a trail that linked several different documents about the topic.

The memex has much in common with today's Web, and perhaps in particular with encyclopedic sites such as the Wikipedia. As Bush wrote, 'Wholly new forms of encyclopedias will appear, ready made with a mesh of associative trails running through them, ready to be dropped into the memex and there amplified' (Bush 1945). However, Bush only imagined the memex as a single-user machine. A memex-user would be able to buy or borrow another person's trails and load them into her own machine, but Bush did not imagine the Web with its networks of interconnected memexes. Although the memex was never built, many people who were later involved in the early development of hypertext read Bush's article and were inspired by it.

The term hypertext was coined in 1965 by Ted Nelson with the following words: 'Let me introduce the word "hypertext" to mean a body of written or pictorial material interconnected in such a complex way that it could not conveniently be presented or represented on paper' (Nelson 1965). At the time, Nelson was a sociology student, but he later became one of the chief visionaries of hypertext. In a later paper, Nelson is more specific in his definition of hypertext, defining it as one kind of hypermedia: ' "Hypertext" means forms of writing which branch or perform on request; they are best presented on computer display screens . . . Discrete, or chunk style, hypertexts consist of separate pieces of text connected by links' (Nelson 1970; see also Wardrip-Fruin 2004 for further discussion of definitions of hypertext). Blogs are what Nelson called discrete, or chunk style, hypertext, although blogs may certainly contain or be part of more complex forms of hypermedia.

At the same time as Nelson began to theorize hypertext, other researchers were developing early hypertext systems. Doug Engelbart's invention of the mouse and the graphical user interface in the 1960s was crucial in this development. Prior to this, all computing was command-line based, so that the user would type in a command and the computer would print a response to a screen or to paper. The technology of the graphical user interface took many years to reach homes. The first personal computers were not available until 1975, and were sold in kits that had to be put together by the owner. They had no screens, but a console of blinking lights. Most of today's computer users would probably not have recognized these computers as personal computers. The first home computer with a graphical user interface and a mouse was not available until Apple's Lisa was released in 1982, followed by the release of the far more popular Macintosh in 1984.

In 1974, before the first home computer was available, Ted Nelson self-published a book that became extremely influential: *Computer Lib/Dream Machines*. In this book, Nelson foresaw a world where everybody could publish and author hypertexts. Ted Nelson insisted that 'You must understand computers now!', and many of his ideas were very close to the Web we know today. Nelson named his imagined network Xanadu, after the place where the pleasure-dome was built in Coleridge's poem 'Kubla Khan'. Xanadu was to have been a network similar to the Internet in that it connected many distributed servers, and in that it would hold an ever-expanding number of documents – the 'docuverse'. Unlike the Web, Xanadu had provisions for copyright and for versioning. It included plans for a system of micro-payments where citations would be tracked. So if I embedded one of your YouTube videos in my blog, for instance, then readers of the blog would automatically be required to make a tiny payment to you every time they viewed the video. There would be no broken links – whereby you follow a link and get an error message because the Web site is no longer active – because every version of every document would have a permanent address and be archived forever. Links would all be bi-directional, so my blog would automatically show you links to every other site that linked to it. In many ways, Xanadu had solutions to problems we're now seeing with the Web – but on the other hand its complexity ensured that it was never fully released. Tim Berners-Lee's World Wide Web, as we discussed in chapter 1, was simple and thus got started.

Visionaries like Ted Nelson, Vannevar Bush and Doug Engelbart have been important not only in the actual development of technology but in our ideas of what the Internet should be. Although Xanadu was never realized, a large portion of the people who were involved in computers in the 1970s and 1980s read and were inspired by Nelson's writings.

The utopias described in this early visionary work have a lot in common with some of the most enthusiastic discussions of blogs today. Yet Nelson realized that a technology like hypertext and communication through a network was not a simple innovation: 'Tomorrow's hypertext systems have immense political ramifications, and there are many struggles to come', Nelson warns (1993, 3/19). As Stuart Moulthrop wrote in 1991:

> Xanadu would remove economic and social gatekeeping functions from the current owners of the means of text production (editors, publishers, managers of conglomerates). It would transfer control of cultural work to a broadly conceived population of culture workers: writers, artists, critics, 'independent scholars,' autodidacts, 'generalists,' fans, punks, cranks, hacks, hackers, and other non- or quasi-professionals. (Moulthrop 1991)

Perhaps if we had realized that that was what Tim Berners-Lee was up to, the Web would not have had such a successful start.

Technological Determinism or Cultural Shaping of Technology?

It would be easy to assume that technology directly affects the social organization of media and communication. Television production studios and printing presses require skill and money to operate, so of course not everyone can have their own television station or run their own newspaper. Since the Web happens to allow far cheaper and less skill-intensive access to publication and distribution, it follows, so we could argue, that the social organization of communication changes in response.

The idea that technology determines social and cultural trends and patterns is known as *technological determinism*, and has often been criticized (Chandler 1996). Although it is clear that technology does affect the ways in which we live, technology does not appear out of a void, and is itself shaped by cultural developments. This more moderate viewpoint has been referred to as *co-construction*, a term that emphasizes the mutual dependencies between technology and culture. It is also important to remember that many of the ways in which we use technology are neither necessary nor obvious. One of the best examples of this is the dominant use of radios in the twentieth century.

Radio technology, which was developed at the very end of the nineteenth century, was first used as a two-way form of communication, a tradition that continued with ham radio. However, most consumer radios are designed as dedicated receivers and cannot be used for transmitting, so for most people radio is a one-way medium. Bertolt Brecht, the influential German playwright who aimed at creating theatre that would make people think critically rather than simply sit back and be entertained, wrote about the potential for a different kind of radio in 1932:

> [R]adio is one-sided when it should be two-. It is purely an apparatus for distribution, for mere sharing out. So here is a positive suggestion: change this apparatus over from distribution to communication. The radio would be the finest possible communication apparatus in public life, a vast network of pipes. That is to say, it would be if it knew how to receive as well as to transmit, how to let the listener speak as well as hear, how to bring him into a relationship instead of isolating him. On this principle the radio should step out of the supply business and organize its listeners as suppliers. Any attempt by the radio to give a truly public character to public occasions is a step in the right direction. (Brecht 1964)

Early radios were generally two-way: they could transmit as well as receive. However, the technology of radio rapidly developed into a mass medium, where a small number of media producers broadcast to a large, mostly passive audience. Ham radio, where everybody is both a sender and a receiver, still exists, but is clearly a marginal activity, in which only a small number of enthusiasts participate. Radios are also used for two-way communication in various professional contexts, such as between police officers, taxi drivers and pilots, but, for most people, radio is a one-way medium.

Brecht's comment shows that radio could have developed differently. Ham radio could have been the dominant medium to come out of the technology of radio transmission, and it could have become what Brecht believed would be 'the finest possible communication apparatus in public life'. Instead, it remained a one-way medium.

Perhaps today's mobile phones are the implementation of Brecht's dream of two-way radio. Radio talk shows do in fact 'organize . . . listeners as suppliers', as Brecht wrote, combining telephone and radio technology by having listeners call in to give their opinions. Telephones without radio, however, primarily allow one-to-one communication, and while this can strengthen existing relationships it doesn't open up new possibilities. I like to imagine that what Brecht was describing was peer-to-peer radio: podcasting.

So why wasn't radio used as a two-way medium? Why didn't it 'let the listener speak as well as hear', and 'bring him into a relationship instead of isolating him'? Why were the twentieth-century media – not just radio, but newspapers, cinema and later television – so dominated by a one-to-many, mass media approach?

Part of the reason why uni-directional mass media dominated was simply cost: it cost a lot to set up a pre-digital printing press or a professional broadcasting studio, and, with traditional technology, specialized technical skills were needed such as filming, editing and typography. A highly professionalized class of journalists and editors developed in parallel. This explanation takes technological limitations as the starting point, adding the issues of socio-economic status and access to money.

Technology was not the only reason, however: legislation limiting broadcasting rights to established players has had just as large an impact on the shaping of the media as has technology. To start a television station in the twentieth century, you didn't simply need skills and equipment – in many countries you also needed a licence from the government to have a frequency allocated to your station. There is a technological side to this: the total number of frequencies that can be used for television and radio broadcast is limited, so the choice to restrict the right to broadcast was a way of managing a scarce resource that was seen to belong to the public. While the early years of radio broadcast in the United States were character-ized by what Andrew Crisell calls 'aerial anarchy' (Crisell 2002, 18), broadcast airwaves have been regulated by the Federal Communications Commission, known as the FCC, since the Communications Act of 1934 (Epstein 1997). In many European countries, regulation was so strict that only a state broadcaster was permitted to use the airwaves. The Norwegian broadcasting monopoly did not end until the 1980s (Bastiansen and Dahl 2003).

There have always been ways of avoiding these regulations. For instance, Radio Luxembourg broadcast in English from Luxembourg on frequencies that were easily received on radios in the United Kingdom and other Western European coun-tries, thus escaping the state monopolies in some of these countries. During the Second World War, radio was an impor-tant way for the resistance movement to communicate with the population. Other, so-called 'pirate radio stations' have broadcast from ships outside of a country's waters or simply used frequencies they were not entitled to use. With the Internet and digital distribution of audio-visual media, the scarcity that led to the regulation of broadcasting no longer exists: simply connect more servers to the network and there will be room for more communication.

Another, more culturally based, argument for why mass media were so dominant is that twentieth-century culture was fixed in the mindset of print, a mindset that is only around 400 years old. A major aspect of the print-based mindset is that cultural expression is something that is produced by an individual or a small group of people, and that, once produced, it is fixed – it doesn't change. Additionally, this product is a commodity that can be sold and that is owned by a person or company. We think of *Romeo and Juliet*, for instance, not simply as a love story about two teenagers, but as a specific text written by Shakespeare. Performances of the play are not seen as the original, they are enactments of the fixed text. Mass media follow this pattern in producing authoritative versions created by a small number of people and spread to large audiences. The exact copies of a television programme that are viewed by millions of people at exactly the same time are equivalent to the identical copies of printed books that are distributed to hundreds or millions of readers.

Blogs and the social publishing and communication forms that have developed on the Web are part of this larger picture of communication and publishing through the ages. They allow more dialogue than the pre-digital written word, and allow even cheaper and more extensive distribution than print or broadcasting. Blogs can be seen as belonging to the post-Gutenberg era, a time after the dominance of print and of mass media. They use technologies first imagined by visionaries of hypertext, but are more social than even these visionaries imagined. In the next chapter, we will focus on the social aspects of blogs and of social networking sites, a kind of communication very closely connected to blogs and that might even be seen as a kind of blogging.

CHAPTER THREE

Blogs, Communities and Networks

Blogs are a social genre. Bloggers don't simply write to their 'Dear Diary', they write into the world with a clear expectation of having readers. That readership does not necessarily need to be very large. On the Internet, everyone is famous to fifteen people, David Weinberger wrote, in a twist on Andy Warhol's familiar line about everyone getting their fifteen minutes of fame (Weinberger 2002, 104). Often, an audience of fifteen close friends, or of fifteen people who are genuinely interested in what you are writing about, is quite sufficient.

Instead of mass communication from a few producers to large, mostly passive audiences, blogs support a dense network of small audiences and many producers. Software built to support such networks of social interactions is called social software.

Blogs are a relatively free-form type of social software, and are decentralized, often running on their author's own domains and connecting haphazardly to other blogs. Social software is often centralized on a single server, like Facebook, Bebo or MySpace, where all users have profiles on the same domain, and the system automatically links to the profiles of the people you've designated as friends. Some blogging sites are also centralized in this way, such as LiveJournal, or blogs hosted on Wordpress.com. Like Facebook or MySpace, these blogging sites will often allow bloggers to mark other bloggers as friends, and may provide limited access to a blog to readers who are not the bloggers' friends. Even blogs that are not part of a centralized site like LiveJournal can, however, be seen as social software, and, though decentralized, blogs certainly map and perform a social network. Usually, this network is most visible though links. Many blogs have blogrolls that provide a list of other blogs the blogger frequents. If the blog allows comments, commentators will generally leave links to their own blogs. Additionally, most blogs also link to conversations that are happening elsewhere, in other blogs.

The links between blogs can be read by computers. Search engines and more specialized services use them to trace the patterns and connections between blogs. Technorati.com is one of the most popular and comprehensive blog search engines. It not only lists the most popular (or at least the most linked-to) blogs, it also allows you to search for any blog or URL and see which other blogs are linking to it. By tracking links from blogs, Technorati provides a tool for following trends. It can show you which YouTube videos are generating the most buzz in the blogosphere by displaying the videos that are receiving the most links at any moment. It does the same for books, movies and other items. Other services visualize the networks between blogs and other Web sites by drawing a map of connections showing sites that are frequently linked to as closer and stronger than sites that are more rarely linked.

These external services provide an *exoskeleton* for blogs, displaying a community between blogs that is not necessarily immediately visible to a casual visitor. A new blogger who doesn't already have connections to other bloggers may find it hard to enter this somewhat implicit social network. Other online communities, such as YouTube, MySpace and Facebook, are gathered on a single site, and can thus immediately provide new bloggers with suggestions as to where friends or potential connections might be. These sites can be said to provide an *intraskeleton* for the social network. More and more of these sites integrate blogs, and an increasing number of people's first experience of blogging is on such sites. Of course, some such sites have been part of blogging since the beginning. LiveJournal has always been a strong, single site for a very large community (or communities) of diarists and bloggers.

Much current research on blogs discusses them in relationship to social networks. Additionally, many of the new ways blogs are being used are closely connected to other uses of social software, where blogs form part of, but not the entirety of, the site. In this chapter I will discuss some of these new ways blogs are evolving and present some important ideas from current research. But first let's look at the background that shapes current theories of social software.

Social Network Theory

A lot of the work on social software builds upon sociological theories of social networks, such as Mark Granovetter's theory of weak ties (1973). Granovetter was interested in how ideas spread through communities, and argued that *weak ties* between individuals are more important than *strong ties* for the broad dissemination of information. His argument is fairly simple (though backed by considerable data and analysis): if A and B know each other very well, and A and C know each other very well, it is highly likely that B and C also know each other. If A needs a job, she'll ask B and C. They probably won't have any new information, because A already shares most of the information that B and C have. There's a far greater chance A will get new information – for instance about a job that might suit her – from her weak ties, that is, from acquaintances and people whom she doesn't see very often. The greater social distance between A and her acquaintance D means that D knows more things that A doesn't already know.

Weak ties are also important because they work as bridges between social groups. People who are bridges between two groups may appear to be socially isolated but actually have weak ties with two or more groups, and these weak ties give them very early access to new information. Granovetter connects this to the 'small world' experiments conducted by Stanley Milgram and his associates (Milgram 1967) and replicated and expanded upon by many researchers since. The experiments are named from the common exclamation 'What a small world!' when people realize they both know the same person. In the experiments, Milgram's team asked participants to send a booklet to a randomly chosen target person by forwarding it to a person they knew who was more likely than themselves to know the target. Although many of the booklets never reached their target and the project had significant problems, the booklets that did attain their goal had an average of six connections in the chain, leading to the popular idea of there being 'six degrees of connection' between any two people in the world. The original study dealt only with people within the United States, and the booklets had to be passed on in person rather than by mail. There are current studies trying to find out whether the phenomenon might exist globally, and in digital forms – how many forwardings of an email does it take for the email to reach a specific person, not known to the original recipient? Back in 1973, however, Granovetter noted that Milgram's studies found that the chain was more likely to be completed if there was a *weak* tie between people in the chain. That is, if a person passed on the booklet to an acquaintance rather than to a family member or close friend, there was a higher chance that it would reach its target, particularly in inter-racial chains.

In terms of social networks, links between blogs can signify that two bloggers know each other and think of each other as friends or acquaintances, but they may also simply signify that one blogger likes reading another blogger's posts. Social networks usually develop for other reasons than pure information gathering, such as family ties, a common job or a shared neighbourhood. Blogs, on the other hand, may exist primarily as networks for sharing ideas, trends and information. Take fashion bloggers, for instance. Fashion bloggers, like Agathe Bjørnsdatter at *Style Bytes*, post photos of their own outfits or of well-dressed people they've seen on the street. They might also share ideas, write about where you can buy certain garments or accessories, post notes and photos from fashion shows or magazines, and comment on trends. Most fashion blogs link to other fashion blogs, sensibly enough, both because these are blogs they read and because their readers are likely to be interested in them. So, by looking at the links between fashion blogs, you can see a map of a social network or community of interest. This is a network not primarily created by family ties or a shared space (school or neighbourhood), as most offline social networks are; this social network is primarily about the sharing of information. The network isn't exclusively about information, of course. Trust is built, as are friendships, alliances and controversies. Trends and styles spread and evolve within the network, not necessarily as something deliberate, but simply in the way certain conventions are likely to arise, in the length of posts, for instance, or in the use of photos, the style of writing or the number of links used. Let's say there are two dozen popular fashion blogs, but the bloggers all go to similar shops, watch the same designers and only read one another's blogs. Remember Granovetter: this is an example of a closed social network, where A and B and C all know each other equally well. Such a network will have difficulty getting new information – unless there are weak links between some of the members of the network and a different network that has access to different information. In such a network, following Granovetter, the most valuable node will be the one that brings in new information through connections with other groups of people.

Distributed Conversations

The Internet was designed as a *distributed* network, where each computer is connected to a number of adjacent computers rather than to a single, central hub. This structure was detailed in an often-cited memorandum, later published as a scientific paper, by Paul Baran (Baran 1964). One of the reasons for Baran's recommendation of a distributed network for the Internet was that such a network was thought to be more likely to remain functional in the case of an attack on it than a

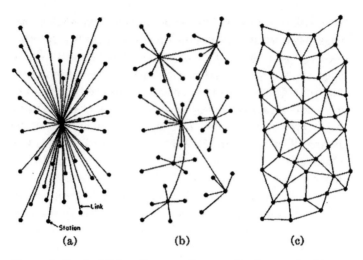

Figure 6: On the left is a diagram of a centralized network where all nodes connect to a single central hub. This structure is also called a star structure. On the right is a diagram of a distributed network, where each node is connected to several adjacent nodes (Baran 1964).

centralized network would be. In a centralized network, the entire network would go down if the central hub malfunctioned.

The relationship between mass media and their readers, listeners or viewers can be compared to such a centralized network, where one central hub connects to many individual nodes, but where nodes cannot connect directly to other nodes. Blogs, on the other hand, are organized as a distributed network. There is no central hub: instead, blogs link to a number of other individual blogs.

The network of blogs isn't equally distributed in the way Baran's network is portrayed in Figure 6. Some Web sites receive far more links from blogs than others. Obvious examples of sites that become hubs in the network of blogs are sites like Technorati, Digg or Blogger, which are all sites that are not themselves blogs but that index blogs, provide general links to popular blogs, or are platforms that people use for blogging.

Individual blogs are not equal nodes in the network either: some are far more popular than others. There are several sites that list the most popular blogs, organized either by number of readers or by the numbers of links pointing to them. It's easier for search engines to count links than to count readers, as information about visitors to a blog is only registered by the server hosting the blog, and so is not publicly available. However, there are rating services, such as Alexa.com, that have volunteers who use their software when they surf the Internet, so that Alexa can see which sites their group of hopefully typical Web users visit most frequently. Based on their statistics, Alexa calculates an approximate number of visitors that major sites likely attract. Links, on the other hand, are easier to count, but do not necessarily translate into visitors.

Go to Technorati's list of the most popular blogs, or to another list of popular blogs, and you will see that there is a vast difference between the popularity of the ten or hundred most popular blogs and that of the tens of thousands that follow. Most blogs only have a handful of other blogs linking to them. These are the 'long tail' of blogging (Anderson 2006). Despite each of these blogs having only a few readers, all of them put together have more than the *New York Times* has readers or the BBC has viewers. At the other end of the spectrum, BoingBoing.net, consistently one of the most linked-to blogs online for the last several years, has 50,000 inbound links.

The vast difference between the most popular blogs and most other blogs can be described by a phenomenon known as the power law (Shirky 2003). Simply put, the power law states that blogs that already have 'power' will get more. Clay Shirky argues that the power law is a common pattern in new social systems such as those we have seen develop online in the last few decades: 'A new social system starts, and seems delightfully free of the elitism and cliquishness of the existing system. Then, as the new system grows, problems of scale set in. Not everyone can participate in every conversation. Not everyone gets to be heard. Some core group seems more connected than the rest of us, and so on' (Shirky 2003). In the blogosphere, power often translates to links. If you have a lot of other bloggers linking to you, your blog will be more easily found not only by the readers of those other blogs who follow the links to your blog, but also by search engines and sites like Technorati, that index links. If I search for 'fashion blog' on Google, the highest hit will be to a site that has a lot of inbound links, because Google sees links as a kind of peer endorsement. The more links, Google's algorithms figure, the better other Internet users must think the site is.

Technology for Distributed Communities

So the connections between blogs can be understood as digitally mediated social networks. How do these networks between blogs develop? How can people talk about blog conversations, or distributed conversations? During a panel discussion at the Media in Transition conference at MIT in April 2007, Cory Ondrejka, who at the time was Chief Technology Officer for the massively multiplayer online world Second Life, argued that community can't develop in blogs, because people aren't present at the same time and in the same place, as they are in a virtual world like Second Life. Blogging, Ondrejka argued, is like standing on a hill yelling into a megaphone. This is much the same argument as Plato made against writing. As we discussed in chapter 2, Plato argued that writing creates a distance between author and reader that does not exist in a conversation, because you can read a text when the author is absent. That distance, Plato argued, made texts unresponsive. If you ask a text a question, it will 'preserve a solemn silence' (Plato 1999). Ondrejka's argument is seen from the perspective of the writer rather than of the reader. If you blog, Ondrejka implies, you're not part of a conversation. You have no immediate access to your readers as you would do in Second Life, a chat room or another synchronous communication space.

On the other hand, what you post in a blog has persistence, whereas a face to face conversation or a conversation in Second Life is usually not archived for future reference.

The present tense is valued in blogs, and it is the most immediately visible aspect of blogs. The most recent post on a blog is always shown first, so a newcomer to a blog will first see what was written today, not necessarily the best post, the most popular post or the post that best represents that particular blog. Technorati disregards links older than six months in its ranking of blog results, and other blog search engines likewise prioritize the new.

Old posts don't simply disappear though. Most blogs automatically archive posts as they get pushed off the front page by newer posts. Archived posts are indexed by search engines, and, while readers who simply type in the URL of a blog are unlikely to come across them, new readers will often find older blog posts about a specific topic when searching for a particular topic.

The archive also allows slow conversations. In real-time or synchronous communication media such as chat rooms, face to face conversations or synthetic worlds (Castronova 2005) such as Second Life or World of Warcraft, participants in the conversation must be present at the same time. If you log onto World of Warcraft five minutes after everybody else in your guild has logged off, you won't only be unable to participate in the discussions they had, you'll have no indication that those discussions ever took place – unless one of your friends logs on and tells you about it, or you read about it on the guild's Web forum or mailing list. Email, Web discussion forums and blogs, on the other hand, are asynchronous media, because participants can communicate with each other without being present at the same time. If you read my blog five minutes after I've published a new post, you'll be able to read my post and see any comments to it.

Conversations between blogs can move quickly, and often the speed of online communication is emphasized. News, popular videos, ideas and images can spread very quickly. One of the advantages of citizen media is this speed. Major events are reported as rapidly by the people who experience them as by mainstream media. Even mainstream media use blog posts published by people who happen to be close to an event. During and after September 11, the tsunami in South-East Asia, hurricane Katrina, the terrorist attacks in London and Madrid, the bombing of Beirut and elections and political events around the globe, bloggers who were present or touched by the events blogged their experiences. For more on this, see chapter 4.

However, the persistence of blog posts – once published, they are generally archived for months or years – means conversations don't necessarily have to take place instantaneously. In fact, Jodi Dean emphasizes the slow pace of conversations in her cluster of theory blogs, where people pick up previous ideas and make connections by linking to older posts in their own or other peoples' blogs, slowly allowing a conversation and interchange of ideas to accumulate. Blogs, she writes, 'are archives, specific accountings of the passage of time that can then be explored, returned to, dug up' (Dean 2006).

To a certain extent, though, Ondrejka has a point when he says blogging is like standing alone on a hill yelling into a megaphone. When you post to your blog, you can't see your readers. Unless you receive comments, it might not be immediately obvious to you whether you even *have* any readers. How on earth do individual blogs, taken together, make a community?

At the base of the network is the simple link. Bloggers read other blogs. If I see something interesting in your blog, I'll likely write a response in my own blog, with a link to your blog so my readers can go and have a look at what you wrote. In addition to allowing human readers to see and follow it, a link is machine readable. For instance, search engines will recognize the link as a connection between our two blogs, and many, such as Google, will interpret the link as me recommending your blog. The more the sites that link to a blog, the higher

Google will rank it in search results. Technorati, the blog search engine, will note that I linked to your blog, and, in addition to adding one to the score of how many blogs link to yours (thus increasing your blog's ranking on their list of popular blogs), Technorati will show my post in its list of blogs linking to yours.

Links are one-way on the World Wide Web, unlike in some earlier hypertext systems. With two-way links, a link from my blog to yours would immediately be visible on both of our blogs. This doesn't happen in basic HTML. However, bloggers can insert code into their Web sites that allows them to track information about their readers. Whenever you visit a Web site, you leave information about your IP number, your screen resolution, which operating system and Web browser you use, and, if you followed a link to get to the Web site, the URL of the Web site you came from. Many bloggers check their Web site statistics daily, tracking how many readers they have and where they come from. This also allows them to see whether readers are coming from new places. If I made a link to your blog, and ten of my readers followed it, you might notice that your Web site statistics show ten more readers than usual, and that they all came from my blog. That would likely make you go and read what I wrote about your blog, and perhaps you would then link back. Today many blogs also support a feature called Trackback. If both my blog and your blog have Trackbacks, my blog will send your blog a 'ping' when I link to you. Your blog will then automatically display a link back to my blog where I wrote about your blog.

Blog search engines also allow bloggers to track conversations between blogs. If I am interested in something you write about in your blog, I might search a blog search engine (such as Technorati or Google's blog search) for the topic, or for blogs that link to your post. If you tagged your post with a keyword, I can easily find other posts on other blogs that are tagged with the same keyword. I might also set up an automatic alert service for certain keywords, such as 'blog conversation', or maybe 'vegetarian sushi recipes' or the name of my favourite rock band. That way, I'd get an email every time a blogger – or a newspaper, depending on how I set up the alert – mentioned those keywords. Finally, bloggers themselves are often the best sources for finding conversations. When I link to your post, I might also link to other bloggers who have written about the same topic. If I have a blogroll, it will list other blogs I enjoy.

Other Social Networks

Blogs are an open network of Web sites that can function as a social network. There are many other social network sites where social connections are even more explicit than in blogs, and these sites have many things in common with blogs. LiveJournal is a site that allows diarists or bloggers to elect to show individual posts to everyone or only to specific groups of their friends. The backbone of LiveJournal is still the journal, where users write blog posts about their daily lives. Other sites, like MySpace, place less emphasis on blogging, making blogging simply a part of users' profiles, which include photos, videos, music they like and various other information about the users' interests. Facebook is another social networking site that has rapidly caught up with MySpace as the most popular site of its kind, although there may be newer and even more popular services by the time you read this book. Facebook was originally only available to college students in the United States, but in late 2006 it was opened up for everyone. When you join Facebook, you connect to one or more networks. While anyone can join a regional network, such as London or Norway, you can only be a member of one regional network at a time. The other form of network you can be a member of is your college, university, high school or workplace, and, to become a member of these, you must have an email address belonging to the appropriate school or workplace. Facebook users can view the profiles of other members of their networks, but can only see the name and profile photo of a user who is not a member of their networks. In September 2007, this basic information also became viewable to users who are not logged in to Facebook, and it is indexed by Google and other search engines. Users are offered the option to opt out of this by choosing a privacy setting, but if the default is full visibility, most users will probably never fiddle with the settings to change this.

If you type a person's name into the search field while you're logged into Facebook, you will see a list of people registered on Facebook who have that name, along with small versions of their profile photos and a note explaining the networks they are a member of. If you are a member of any of these peoples' networks, you will be able to click through and view other information they have added to their profiles. Otherwise, the only way you can read more about them is if you and they mutually agree to be 'friends'. If you do so, other users will be able to see that you are friends, and you will be notified about each other's activities on Facebook.

So where blog communities are not immediately visible to casual observers, social networks of friends on social network sites like Facebook and MySpace are predefined according to traditional ideas of social networks: your connections are the people you go to school with, work with, or live near. Bloggers create communities by linking to each other, by adding each other to their blogrolls and by commenting on each other's sites. On Facebook the same is achieved by adding someone to your friends' list. By adding friends who are not in my work, school or regional networks I can create my own social network, combining weak with strong ties.

There is a number of blog-like qualities to Facebook. As on LiveJournal or MySpace, users may create their own blog posts in Facebook, but this feature is not very heavily used. However, every time you make a change to your profile, write on a friend's profile, join a group, say you'll attend an event, upload a photo, add a new friend or perform various other actions, a news item is automatically generated and added to the top of your profile. This is in a sense an automatically generated blog, where your story is reported or narrated by Facebook itself rather than by you.

Your news items are archived in much the same manner as blog posts are, and visitors to your Facebook profile can click on a link to 'See All' your 'Stories', as events on Facebook are called. They can even choose to read only particular strands of your Facebook activities, choosing, say, only your 'Event Stories', or, more salaciously, your 'Relationship Stories', which report on when you changed your relationship status on your Facebook profile – from 'Single' to 'In a Relationship' for instance, also giving the name of the person you said you were 'In a Relationship' with, if he or she is also on Facebook and has confirmed to Facebook's automated system that the two of you really are 'In a Relationship'.

When you log on to Facebook, your home page is not your own profile, but a page that collates news feeds from all your friends. So you will see new photos uploaded by your friends, comments they have added to discussions and whether they're still dating the person they were dating last week. This news feed may, for instance, look something like this:

> Jane Doe wrote on Vasya Pupkin's wall:
> 'How was your trip? Missed you.'
> Joe Blow and Kari Nordmann are now friends.
> Vasya Pupkin is finally home from Moscow.
> Ola Nordmann and Kari Nordmann are now listed as Married.

When this public collation of news feeds was introduced in 2006, users were so upset that they staged organized protests against it. Facebook has kept the news feeds despite this, but allows users to opt out of sharing their feeds.

Remember the imagined group of fashion bloggers we talked about earlier? If they all only linked to each other, they would be a closed network. In order to gain access to new information, members of the network need to have connections outside of the group. On Facebook, such a spread of information becomes very visible through the news feed. I live in Norway, so I'm a member of the Norway network, and a large proportion of my Facebook friends are Norwegian. A lot of the items I'll see on my news feed when I log on are Norwegian. I see my Norwegian friends joining groups that reference current political or cultural events in Norway, or discussing local issues. On Facebook, a common way of marking identity and personal choices and preferences is by joining – or leaving – a group with a descriptive title. Every time you join or leave a group, the fact will be announced to all your friends: 'Joe joined the group Peace On Earth Now!'; 'Jane joined the group Obama for President!'; 'Jack joined the group Enough with all this politics, let's just party.'

I saw a very concrete example of how news spreads differently in different networks in the days following the college shootings at Virginia Tech in April 2007. Although the story was well covered in the Norwegian mass media, it was experienced by most Norwegians as very distant. Students and lecturers at the university I work at didn't talk about it much, and I saw no mention of it on Facebook among my Norwegian friends. However, many of my Facebook friends are not Norwegian, and so my news feed showed me how my US friends were joining groups in support of the Virginia Tech victims, posting icons to show their grief and writing status messages and notes clearly showing they were thinking of little but the shootings – and small wonder, for the shocking event was far closer to them than to most Norwegians, with many of them knowing people at Virginia Tech. When I delved more deeply into how the shootings were affecting Facebook communities, it became clear that the system of limiting access to networks you're not a member of makes much of what is happening in other networks, invisible to most users. Searching for 'Virginia Tech' and similar keywords revealed a large number of groups dedicated to discussing the massacre, but very few of these were accessible to me, as I was not a member of the networks the groups had been created in. The groups in support of the victims were limited to a single college network, so they would not be accessible to users outside of that college. You would see that the group existed, though, if you had a friend at that college who had joined it: 'Jason has joined the group <u>In Support of Virginia Tech</u>.'

There are many other social networking sites. While Facebook is primarily aimed at and used by students, LinkedIn is a popular social networking site for business people. LinkedIn has a more serious and business-like tone than Facebook, and instead of setting up a profile with photos, friends and hobbies, you enter your CV in careful categories: education, honours, jobs. Instead of 'friends', you have 'connections', and you can write and request recommendations of your work from your connections. Jobs are advertised on LinkedIn, and the idea is that you can find people to hire, work for or collaborate with by browsing through your connections and their connections. Many other Web sites, such as Flickr or LiveJournal, use social networks as a way of organizing another activity, where you are shown your friends or family's photos or blog posts, and can share content with your social network rather than with the entire world.

One of the reasons social networking sites are popular is that they appeal to our instinct for collecting. New media scholar Lisbeth Klastrup reviewed LinkedIn as though it were a computer game in a post to her blog on 19 August 2006:

> Objective of game: You can go either for the single-player mode: to gather as many connections as you can, in the shortest time possible and reach the 100% network cap (state of progress helpfully depicted in the 'network' stat-bar); or the multi-player mode: to gather more 'people in my network' than your fellow players.

Even social networking sites without any clear purpose apart from collecting as many friends as possible have become popular, at least for a while. Orkut, a project coming out of Google, was an example of this. Orkut was one of the first social networking sites, and rapidly became popular among bloggers after its launch in 2004, only to be largely abandoned by them a few months later, when new sites turned up. Perhaps simply seeing photos of all your friends' faces gathered on one page was a feature so satisfying that people would sign up and do it for no other reason. Orkut is also an interesting example of how the demographics of a social networking site can drastically shift. Although the early adopters were mostly Americans and other English-speakers, within months of its launch Brazilian users had outnumbered the Americans two to one. Because the Brazilians wrote in Portuguese, and because messages are broadcast widely on Orkut, this led to the English-speakers complaining about the onslaught of non-English-speakers (Alerigi 2004). It subsequently became popular in Iran, before being banned by the Iranian government – because the dating and matchmaking were at odds with Muslim culture, the government said, though others claimed it was because Orkut allowed users to send messages to large numbers of people at once and easily share information.

Once enough of your friends have joined a social network site, social pressure can make it very difficult *not* to participate. Around 85 per cent of all college students in the United States were on Facebook in September 2005, according to Chris Hughes, a Facebook employee, who gave an interview published on the blog *TechCrunch* on 7 September that year. That is an astounding market penetration. Since Facebook has opened up to non-US residents, other countries' student and non-student populations are rapidly following suit. Some students complain that so much of their social life is organized or happens on Facebook that not to participate is to be socially ostracized. Perhaps, though, Facebook and similar systems provide sites for social interaction that might not take place without the Internet. In Norway, surveys have shown that students have spent less time on campus during the last five to ten years, whether due to an increased need for paid employment to finance their studies or for other reasons. This means they have less interaction with other students than previously.

Facebook and other online social networking tools may help students to maintain the social connections with peers that are crucial for creating a strong learning environment. Not all university and college administrations have looked at Facebook in such a positive light, however. On finding that students spend more time on Facebook than on using the official online learning environments, some campuses have blocked access to Facebook, so students cannot connect to the Web site from the campus network (Fort 2005). Georgetown Visitation, a girls' high school near Washington DC, reportedly not only blocked access to Facebook from the school network but also tried to frighten students away from the site:

> 'Our school is really interested in its image – they don't want us to be given a bad name,' says Katie, a Visitation student. She says the school brought in a law-enforcement officer, who told students that 'by having a Facebook profile we are jeopardizing our future husbands' political careers.' (Rich 2007)

One hopes the girls also consider their own future political careers. More sensible attempts to educate teenagers about the potential dangers of Facebook and blogging include discussing the dangers of revealing personal information about yourself online, and educating students about how easy it is to stalk a person on the basis of the information they blithely share online (Rich 2007). Despite schools' attempts to block Facebook, censorship is very difficult to sustain and can be circumvented with fairly minimal knowledge. For instance, students can use a proxy server to access blocked services rather than connecting directly through the campus network.

As we put more and more of our lives online, privacy issues become an increasing concern. Cory Doctorow's short story 'Scroogled' portrays one possible future scenario where the massive amounts of data stored about individuals by Google and other Web sites provide a means for an oppressive government to control its people (Doctorow 2007). Doctorow's imagined world may not be that distant. There have already been several cases where immigration officers have Googled people upon their arrival in a country, and where seemingly unimportant information is used against them (Elatrash 2007). At the beginning of 'Scroogled', Doctorow quotes Cardinal Richelieu, who wrote in seventeenth-century France: 'Give me six lines written by the most honorable of men, and I will find an excuse in them to hang him.' While most of what we enter into Facebook may seem harmless, we should consider that it could be used in other contexts. Most users are also not aware that uploading photos, videos or writing any message on Facebook gives Facebook the right to use those contributions in any way Facebook sees fit. As of October 2007, Facebook's Terms of Use include the following clause:

> By posting User Content to any part of the Site, you automatically grant, and you represent and warrant that you have the right to grant, to the Company an irrevocable, perpetual, non-exclusive, transferable, fully paid, worldwide license (with the right to sublicense) to use, copy, publicly perform, publicly display, reformat, translate, excerpt (in whole or in part) and distribute such User Content for any purpose on or in connection with the Site or the promotion thereof, to prepare derivative works of, or incorporate into other works, such User Content, and to grant and authorize sublicenses of the foregoing.

The Terms of Use do continue by saying that if the user deletes said content, the licence expires; however, Facebook may still keep archives. A blogger has far greater ownership of his or her own creations, especially if the blog is on an independent server and not hosted by a company such as Blogger.com, which is owned by Google.

Publicly Articulated Relationships

There is a performance aspect to social networking sites that is also present in blogs, though it may be a little more subtle in the latter. When we blog or use social networking sites, we not only present ourselves as individuals, we also publicly proclaim our relationships. On LinkedIn, having influential or well-known connections is as important as having an impressive CV – or at least that is what the interface of the Web site implicitly tells us.

danah boyd, who deliberately does not capitalize her name (boyd 2001), is one of the most prominent researchers of social networking sites, both through her popular blog *Apophenia* and through her research for Berkeley, the MacArthur Foundation and others. boyd uses the term *publicly articulated relationships* to describe the importance of this public display of your social network. She identifies four characteristics of online social spaces that make them fundamentally different from offline social spaces (2007):

1. Persistence
2. Searchability
3. Replicability
4. Invisible audiences

Blogs and social networking sites are *persistent* in that the information you enter is recorded and can be accessed later. From offline spaces, such as a café where we're chatting with friends over cups of coffee, we're used to informal social conversations being ephemeral. We may remember what happened and who said what, or tell each other stories about what happened, but the details are rarely directly accessible. What you blog or talk about on MySpace or Facebook will stick around, unless you work to delete it, and deleting doesn't always work. Online spaces are *searchable*: people can find you. Your mother or boss can find you as easily as your high-school buddies can. These spaces are *replicable*: photos and conversations can be copied and modified so there's no way of telling them apart from the original. This is a tactic often used in bullying, but also in political speech, as when political ads or television interviews are altered to make a political argument. Finally, online spaces have *invisible audiences*. You don't know exactly who is viewing your profile or reading your blog. You can't see the audience as you can when you're speaking to friends at a party or in an offline public space. That means that your conversation with a friend about a party you were at last night might be read by your mother or teacher as well as by your friends. Additionally, because your blog or activities on a social network site are persistent (the first characteristic), some of your audience will be in the future, accessing your photos, words and activities in a quite different context from that in which you originally posted them.

Teens and other users of social networking sites are, boyd argues, aware of these characteristics of online spaces, and are generally adept at navigating them.

Colliding Networks

One danger of online social networks is their visibility – in some cases, they work too well. When bloggers are fired for what they write in their blogs, or teenage daughters are uncomfortable about their mothers joining Facebook, the problem is that two social networks that are meant to be separate collide. danah boyd and Jeffrey Heer have pointed out that in offline environments we usually keep different groups of associates apart through 'a segmentation of place' (boyd and Heer 2006). We meet our boss at work and our friends and family at home. We don't invite our parents to wild parties. boyd has conducted some of her research on an early and very popular social networking site called Friendster. She describes how, as the site became more and more popular, more of these social spheres collided, leading people to tame their profiles to make them more acceptable to a diverse group of people. But, however moderate your profile is, if your friends' profiles are not, and if your friends have left less than tame messages (called testimonials on Friendster) on your profile page, your boss or potential mother-in-law is still going to be shocked when they see your profile. If you stop linking to your friends, there's no point in being on Friendster at all. boyd and Heer present a story that provides a vivid example of this kind of collision between social spheres:

> The dilemma of collapsed contexts and unknown audiences can best be illustrated through the story of a 26-year-old teacher in San Francisco. She created her Profile when all of her Burner friends joined the service. After a group of her students joined the service, they approached her to question her about her drug habits and her friendship with a pedophile. Although her Profile had no reference to drugs or even to Burning Man, many of her friends had both. Furthermore, one of her friends had crafted a Profile that contained an image of him in a Catholic schoolgirl uniform with Testimonials referencing his love of small girls. While his friends knew this to be a joke, the teacher's students did not. The teacher was faced with an impossible predicament. If she removed her Profile or disconnected to her friends, she admitted guilt. Yet, there was no change she could make to her Profile and it was inappropriate to ask her friends to change theirs. Although teachers keep strict physical distance from their students during off-hours, it may prove impossible to maintain a similar distance in online environments. (boyd and Heer 2006)

This negotiation of multiple audiences who know you in very different contexts is also familiar to many bloggers, and is the cause of many unhappy stories. Blogging and participating in social software sites often feel like participating in an intimate conversation – one may be 'famous to fifteen people', to quote David Weinberger again, but, really, fifteen people don't sound very intimidating or a large enough audience to really worry about. However, the fifteen people who read your blog or Facebook profile today will probably not be its only readers. Digital documents tend to stay around for a long time. They are, as danah boyd notes, persistent. You might delete your blog, but it will remain for days or weeks in Google's cache, and unless you've expressly requested it be deleted, it will be probably be archived in several versions at archive.org and

possibly at other sites as well. Those words you wrote when
you were eighteen and furious at your boyfriend, or when you
were twenty-six and hated your job, might come back to haunt
you later, when they're read by somebody you might not even
have known when you wrote the post. Perhaps your future
mother-in-law or children will read what you wrote.

Closer to home, perhaps, are the cases of bloggers who have
been fired because of writing indiscrete blog posts about their
jobs – as, you'll remember from chapter 1, happened to Dooce.
Dooce worked in a technology company and hated it – and
wrote funny but venomous blog posts describing why she
hated it so, such as this one, written on 12 February 2002:

> I hate that one of the 10 vice-presidents in this 30-person
> company wasn't born with an 'indoor' voice, but with a shrill,
> monotone, speaking-over-a-passing-F16 outdoor voice. And
> he loves to hear himself speak, even if just to himself. He
> loves to use authoritative expressions such as 'NO! NO! NO!
> IT'S LIKE THIS!'

The post, which is still online, continued in this vein for several paragraphs, describing a variety of her co-workers and
generally leaving the reader to wonder why she still worked for
these people. Whether Dooce at the time considered the possi-
bility of her co-workers and boss reading these posts is an open
question, but at any rate, shortly after posting the above quote,
she was called in to her boss's office and fired.

Despite the media attention that mishaps such as Dooce's
receive, being fired for your blog is really a rather rare occur-
rence, and avoiding it simply requires that you refrain from
writing things about your job that you wouldn't be happy for
your boss to hear or to see printed in a newspaper. Using a
pseudonym provides an added level of security for those who
really don't want their social spheres to collide, or you can use
services that provide levels of privacy so that posts are not
public to the world. Facebook allows this, but not in a very
nuanced way. LiveJournal, on the other hand, allows users to
specify as many different groups of friends as they like, and

each post in a user's LiveJournal can be set as visible to as many or as few groups of friends as the user likes. That would keep Dooce's boss or the students of the San Francisco teacher away from conversations that were meant to be between friends.

Emerging Social Networks

Although blogs and social networks appear to have developed into fairly stable forms, twenty years hence it may be clear that they were only an early stage, leading to something we don't yet know the nature of. Blogs and social networking sites are both very new forms. It took half a century after Gutenberg invented the printing press for the conventions of print that we today take for granted to be set: early printers did not see page numbers, titles, tables of contents and the like as immediately obvious. Likewise, early cinema was an experimental phase and it took decades before the feature film was an established genre.

Already, there are many new kinds of personal publication tools that are similar to blogs. Facebook's automated news feed is one example, but there are many others. Nokia's Lifelog promises to convert media created or received on your mobile phone and to organize it as an automatically generated diary that you could keep private on your own computer, or upload to the Web as a blog. Items that might be included in your Lifelog would be photos and videos you'd taken on your phone, text and multi-media messages you'd sent or received, events you'd recorded in the calendar on your phone and location data connected to each of these. Few of us would want to upload every item in our Lifelog for public perusal on the Internet, but the software does clearly demonstrate how more and more of a life is being documented today – some of it deliberately, as when you take a photo, and some coincidentally, as when your phone remembers that you sent an SMS, or your computer archives old emails.

Another Web site, Plazes.com, tracks where users are. Registered users at Plazes have set their computers to automatically send Plazes a message every time their computer is registered at a new IP address. Users type in the name of the location (home, office, Paris, New York) and the system generates a chronology of a user's movements, displaying them to the community at large or just to the user's friends, according to the privacy settings the user has selected. If you use a laptop computer both at home and at work and connect it to wireless networks at both places, this may result in nothing more than a fairly innocuous narrative: Thursday at 08:34: Jill is at home. Thursday at 09:27: Jill is at work. Thursday at 17:51: Jill is at home. But if you travel, or connect to the net at a friend's house or at a different café than usual, your friends will know about that too. Plazes thus generates an automated blog about a particular aspect of your life.

Google and other search engines also track your online activities. When you visit a Web site, your browser tells the computer your IP number, and from that, your approximate location can usually be seen – at the least, your IP number announces which ISP you are using. If you're online from a university, your IP number contains information on which university you're at, and sometimes even the specific room you're sitting in. Google stores information that connects search terms to IP numbers, and may use this information in its algorithms. Due to complaints from the EU that this is in conflict with privacy legislation and data protection laws, Google recently announced that they would 'anonymize' this information after eighteen months, presumably retaining the information that a computer at the same IP address searched for, say, 'Nokia lifelog', 'dooced' and 'fired for blogging' on the same afternoon, but removing the exact IP number that conducted the search.

If you sign up for an account with Google, thus giving it more information about yourself, it will in return give you access to the information it stores about you. You can browse back through its chronological list of what you searched for at what time, and note trends in your own obsessions and interests through days, weeks and years. If you install a special toolbar in your browser, you can even opt to tell Google about every single Web site you ever visit, and Google will use that information to customize your search results, attempting to find you exactly the things that it knows you like to see.

When a piece of software – Google, Plazes, a Nokia phone or Facebook – presents such traces of your life in chronological order, those traces become an extended narrative, an autobiography created on the fly. This is an automatically generated autobiography, though. You wrote it – after all, you were the one who did those things, and you knew they were being recorded – but you didn't shape its narration.

In some ways, this automated diarying highlights the ways that self-documentation has always been both incidental and deliberate. Before digital cameras, people often kept their never-sorted photos in shoeboxes, along with other paraphernalia of their daily lives: tickets from trips they'd taken or shows they'd been to, cuttings from newspapers and so on. Only some of these would make it into photo albums and scrapbooks or be written about in diaries. Today's technology can write a story automatically from all these scraps of information about ourselves. Whether or not we want our stories told like this is another matter.

Imagine a complete story of every technologically mediated event in your life – every photo taken of you or by you, every phone call you've made, every email you've sent, everything you've ever written on a computer, every time you checked your email from a different computer, every game you've played. You reached level 70 in World of Warcraft on 14 May 2007; your best score in online scrabble was 361 points, on 21 January 2006; here's that conversation on the webcam with your niece on her second birthday, and the SMS your friend sent you when her boyfriend broke up with her. Your computer would organize all this for you in the same way that Facebook organizes your relationship stories and event stories. You could choose to publish parts of your story online, as a blog that you share with others. Perhaps some sections are only available to certain people, just as you, a generation ago, might have had some photo albums that you would only show to certain friends. Today you could nearly do this on Facebook, although it would be a lot of work as you'd have to manually upload each document, and there isn't a lot of nuance in deciding who would have access to what. And Facebook would own all your content. If they go bankrupt, it would be lost. If they were sold, someone else would own your life story, and maybe they'd use it in ways you wouldn't like. An alternative might be an open access, distributed social network system. In such a system, you'd host your own Web site with your own documents, posts, photos and videos, but encoded in your site you'd have information about who could access what, and about who else would be interested in which things. So you could easily let your sister have access to the recording of your latest phone conversation with her, and so on.

Would we want to do this? Where will systems like Facebook and blogs go in the future? Will our ability to document everything lead to us actually doing so? Participating in these kinds of auto-tracking social networks means giving up a large portion of our privacy, something we seem to be more and more complacent about doing. Perhaps that is because the return is so great: a stronger sense of belonging to a community, of belonging to a group of people who not only see who we are, but who care about us as well.

CHAPTER FOUR

Citizen Journalists?

In the middle of the twentieth century, the journalist Abbott Joseph Liebling wrote a sentence that has often been quoted since: 'Freedom of the press is guaranteed only to those who own one' (Liebling 1960). Although freedom of speech was recognized as an important human right in the twentieth century, in practice only a tiny percentage of the population in twentieth-century democracies could easily share their ideas with more than the people immediately surrounding them. Listener and reader contributions to mainstream media such as television, radio and newspapers existed but were always positioned in carefully boundaried spaces. In talkback radio programmes listeners could call in their questions but would often be cut off if they said anything too controversial or rude. Letters to the editor wouldn't always be published and would always remain clearly subordinate to the editorial content of the newspaper.

In twentieth-century democratic societies, people wishing to have their words and ideas published or broadcast had to contend with editorial policies that were generally based on ideology or on what advertisers would support or the public buy. In such a media landscape, many stories would never be deemed 'newsworthy' enough to be heard. In non-democratic societies, censorship and ideological suppression by the state stopped other kinds of stories from reaching an audience. In either case, those who did not, as Liebling wrote, own a press were not able to spread their ideas. Despite the existence of underground media consisting of pirate radio stations, zines, photocopied newsletters and other oppositional or small-scale, non-commercial media outlets, the mainstream media's domination of the airwaves and distribution outlets made this media subculture invisible to most people.

The Internet changed one of the greatest obstacles to true freedom of the press by eliminating or greatly reducing the cost of production and distribution. By the end of the century, bloggers *could*, in effect, own a press: a modern, lightweight version of one. Blogs provide a means of publishing and distributing that is cheap and simple enough for everyone in the Western world to use directly, whether from home, school, the library or even a mobile phone.

This new freedom to publish at will has caused journalists and editors to reevaluate the role of mainstream, professional media. If you want more information about a current event today, you can easily search across blogs, newspapers and other sources, finding stories far more diverse and extensive than those traditionally printed in a newspaper or relayed on the television news. If you're interested in the US elections, you can directly access blogs written by the candidates and their staff, you can read transcripts or videos of debates between decision makers, and opinions from knowledgeable or simply opinionated bloggers. If you're interested in the situation in the Middle East, you can not only find extensive material from politicians and political parties, you can also read the diaries of people experiencing the conflicts here and now. Nobody will vet these diaries as newsworthy or not, there is no editor deciding which diary entries to publish – although social networks and automated indexes will make some more visible than others, as will be discussed later in this chapter.

As blogs became a familiar genre, the mainstream media began to discuss whether blogging was a threat to journalism and to the media as we have known them throughout the twentieth century. Journalists began to ask a question that kept recurring: is blogging journalism? The answer is obviously usually no: most blogs are not journalism, nor do their writers aspire to be journalists. However, whether or not individual

blogs can be thought of as journalism, blogs and other participatory media are changing the ways journalism works.

This chapter will examine three general ways in which blogs
intersect with journalism. First, blogs can give first-hand
reports from ongoing events, whether wars, natural disasters
or crimes. Sometimes bloggers merely stumble across some
event that turns out to be of greater interest, and they are
chance witnesses. The more moving and influential blogs in
these areas are, however, usually those where the blogger is a
participant in the ongoing events, such as in the case of the
Baghdad civilians and US soldiers who blogged during the
Iraq war, or the inhabitants of New Orleans who blogged
during hurricane Katrina.

Second, some bloggers set out to tell stories that might just
as well have been told by traditional journalists – but where
mainstream media have either failed to investigate an issue
critically enough or where the story is not deemed fitting or of
sufficient interest to be publicized. These bloggers may pool
resources and track down details in a way that many professional journalists do not have the time for. In these cases, blogs
fulfil much the same function as journalists do. In some cases,
blogs provide independent-minded journalists with a printing
press of their own, free of any editor, as when Christopher
Allbritton travelled to Iraq as an independent journalist, completely funded by the donations of his readers.

Third, many bloggers follow mainstream media and other
blogs and filter stories according to their interests, or they carefully monitor every news item about a particular person or
issue. These bloggers are often called filterbloggers, but have
also been called *gatewatchers* by Axel Bruns (2005). Bloggers
thus represent a turn, from the gatekeeping that the mass
media has traditionally performed, to gatewatching, as we'll
examine in more detail later in this chapter.

Before looking at examples of these three ways in which blogging can approach journalism, we will look at surveys showing
how bloggers themselves see their blogging in relationship to

journalism. We will also consider a central tenet of journalism, the expectation that journalists are reliable and tell the truth objectively, as this is a crucial way in which bloggers, with their subjective point of view, tend to differ from journalists.

Bloggers' Perception of Themselves

Most bloggers do not think of themselves as journalists. In fact, in a July 2006 survey of American bloggers by Pew Internet Research, 65 per cent of those interviewed stated that they did not think of their blogging as a form of journalism (Lenhart and Fox 2006). This survey was unusual by being nationally representative. Most surveys of bloggers find their sample online, for instance by choosing to look at all blogs that link to a certain blog, or at blogs by people who respond to a question-naire published online. These methods make it difficult to be certain that the sample chosen is representative, as the bloggers either are self-selected or show only a small area of the blogos-phere. Because bloggers tend to read and link to other blogs that are similar to their own, it is easy to develop a skewed view of what the 'typical' blogger might be like, and this has led to several false debates. For instance, a regularly occurring dis-cussion in the blogosphere concerns the perceived lack of women bloggers. Surveys show that there is a fairly even gender balance. In 2003 Susan Herring and her research group found that 48 per cent of bloggers in their sample were women and 52 per cent were men. Blogs hosted on typical journaling sites like LiveJournal and DiaryLand were excluded from the sample, as were blogs that had not been updated in the last two weeks. The selection was taken from the random function of blo.gs, a blog tracking service (Herring et al. 2004). In 2006, using a somewhat different methodology, researchers from Pew Internet Research found that 46 per cent of bloggers were women and 54 per cent men (Lenhart and Fox 2006). Both sur-veys demonstrate that any perceived gender imbalance must be a perception rather than based on objective data.

Herring argues that the reason for the impression that there are more male bloggers is the emphasis in the media on filter blogs, which Herring's survey found to be predominantly written by adult males. However, Herring's group found that only 13 per cent of all blogs are filter blogs or knowledge blogs, a category Herring defines as 'repositories of information and observations with a typically technological focus'. Forty per cent of journal- or diary-style bloggers are men, so this style of blogging is not dominated by women. The effect, however, of the media and the focus of scholarship on male-dominated filter blogs is, as Herring writes, that 'actual diversity (and hence evidence of the democratic nature of weblogs) is discursively minimized' (Herring et al. 2004).

It has also often been noted that male bloggers tend to link more to other men than they do to women bloggers. That means that, for people who mostly read men's blogs, it might look as though there are 'no women bloggers', while the reality is that they are simply less visible within certain groups of blogs. To solve the problem of characterizing the actual blogosphere rather than an individual's impression of it, Pew Internet Research dialled random Americans and asked whether they blogged. Then the surveyors continued by surveying only the respondents who said that they were bloggers.

The Pew researchers took their question one step further by also asking whether the bloggers 'engage in practices generally associated with journalism: directly quoting sources, fact checking, posting corrections, receiving permission to post copyright material and linking to original source materials out of the blog' (11). They found that about a third of bloggers say they 'often' try to verify facts before publishing them and that they try to link to their sources, while a little over 20 per cent 'sometimes' do so. The other activities are less frequent. This means that, although only 34 per cent of bloggers think of their blogging as a form of journalism, nearly 60 per cent of them in fact 'often' or 'sometimes' try to verify facts and reference their sources. It should also be noted that 37 per cent of the bloggers surveyed said that the main topic of their blog was 'my life and personal experiences' (9) – these are diary-style blogs, and so fact-checking and linking original sources would be entirely irrelevant. Only 5 per cent of the bloggers in the survey focused on the typically journalistic topics of news and current events (Lenhart and Fox 2006).

When it Matters Whether a Blogger is a Journalist

You don't need a particular degree or licence to call yourself a journalist, as you would to call yourself a doctor or a psychologist. Instead, you call yourself a journalist if you work as a journalist. Until very recently, that meant that you published your writing in a newspaper or that you worked in television or radio. Today, this may also mean that you are a blogger – but if it does, that means it is much harder than previously to determine whether or not an individual is a journalist. Usually it really doesn't matter, but sometimes the distinction can be very important – legally or pragmatically.

On an everyday level, as blogging has become recognized as an important part of the media ecology, bloggers have been more likely to receive passes to press conferences and political conventions, which allow the bloggers to report first-hand on these events rather than leaving them to rely on reports from traditional journalism. At a more dramatic level, whether or not a person is seen as a 'journalist' can be a very important legal distinction. This has been most clearly tested in the United States, where journalists in many states have the right to protect their sources' anonymity, even in a court of law. Such so-called 'shield' laws vary in degree from state to state, but are often seen to be an important prerequisite for freedom of speech, because, without such protection, many people would not feel safe speaking to journalists about contentious issues. In 2004, bloggers' right to withhold the identity of their sources, as journalists may do, was tested when a group of bloggers published information about products Apple was planning to release. Apple sued 'John Does', that is, the unknown people whom Apple assumed had leaked Apple's trade secrets to the bloggers. Apple then claimed that the bloggers who had published the information were legally required to identify their sources, and thus reveal who the 'John Does' were. The bloggers argued that their anonymous sources were protected because they were acting as journalists, but Apple argued that they were not journalists and that the confidentiality of media sources was therefore not legally privileged. The Electronic Frontier Foundation took the part of the bloggers and eventually won the court case (Electronic Frontier Foundation 2006).

On its Web site, The Electronic Frontier Foundation states that it is 'battling for legal and institutional recognition that if you engage in journalism, you're a journalist, with all of the attendant rights, privileges, and protections'. Unfortunately it is not easy to define unequivocally what it means to 'engage in journalism'.

Recently proposed legal definitions show the shift that is occurring in our understanding of what a journalist is. In the United States, several drafts of the Free Flow of Information Bill, which is intended to protect free speech by permitting journalists to shield their sources, have been discussed. In a 2005 draft, people to be protected in this way were defined exclusively according to the medium in which the person published, which was required to be:

> (A) an entity that disseminates information by print, broadcast, cable, satellite, mechanical, photographic, electronic, or other means and that –
> (i) publishes a newspaper, book, magazine, or other periodical in print or electronic form;
> (ii) operates a radio or television broadcast station (or network of such stations), cable system, or satellite carrier, or a channel or programming service for any such station, network, system, or carrier; or

(iii) operates a news agency or wire service;

(B) a parent, subsidiary, or affiliate of such an entity to the extent that such parent, subsidiary, or affiliate is engaged in news gathering or the dissemination of news and information; or

(C) an employee, contractor, or other person who gathers, edits, photographs, records, prepares, or disseminates news or information for such an entity. (US Congress 2005)

A later draft of the bill, the Free Flow of Information Act of 2006, proposed a definition that is significantly broader, and that interestingly enough is not tied to a specific medium:

a person who, for financial gain or livelihood, is engaged in gathering, preparing, collecting, photographing, recording, writing, editing, reporting, or publishing news or information as a salaried employee of or independent contractor for a newspaper, news journal, news agency, book publisher, press association, wire service, radio or television station, network, magazine, Internet news service, or other professional medium or agency which has as one of its regular functions the processing and researching of news or information intended for dissemination to the public. (US Congress 2006)

While it is usually unimportant whether we regard a blogger as a journalist or not, there are times when it really matters. These legal definitions show that blogging and other forms of user-created media are causing us to redefine the nature of journalism itself. It remains to be seen whether legal definitions of journalism and blogging are necessary in other countries.

Objectivity, Authority and Credibility

Journalism is expected to be objective and reliable, and the editor and the brand of the newspaper or broadcast medium itself stand as guarantees of this. Journalists are also afforded certain protections, such as (in some countries) the right to preserve the anonymity of their sources. Blogs, on the other hand, are subjective and independent, and come with no guarantee of truth, and do not necessarily have the same rights as traditional media. Geert Lovink describes it thus: 'There is a quest for truth in blogging. But it is a truth with a question mark. Truth here has become an amateur project, not an absolute value, sanctioned by higher authorities' (Lovink 2007b, 13)

Interestingly enough, a survey of blog readers by the advertising company Blogads showed that they visit blogs precisely because they see them as more credible than mainstream media (Blogads 2004). In this survey, 61.4 per cent of respondents stated that they read blogs because there was 'more honesty', while 50.3 per cent found the 'transparent biases' of blogs an important factor in their choice to read blogs. By traditional standards, that seems counter-intuitive indeed. How could an individual writer with no credentials be more credible than a professionally trained journalist writing for a well-established publication with a staff of editors and fact-checkers, and, not least, a reputation to protect? Melissa Wall argues that bloggers, like mainstream media, have ways of building trust and credibility, but that these techniques are not the same:

> Just as mainstream media establish a pattern of routines to create a sense of dependability, so many of these sites seem to rely on their own distance from power for their credibility. What is notable here is that credibility seems to be established in part by characteristics that are quite different from the traditional. Many of these blogs seem to turn conventional wisdom upside down – the more personal and more open about opinions a site is, the more trustworthy and credible it will be. (Wall 2005, 165)

Blogs rely on personal authenticity, whereas traditional journalism relies on institutional credibility. We trust or distrust an article in a newspaper on the basis of our perception of the newspaper, which is partly shaped by the society around us and partly by our own personal knowledge of the newspaper. Who the reporter is sometimes matters, but primarily it is the reputation of the media outlet that is important. Most of us are more likely to trust a news story we have read in the *Guardian* or the *New York Times* or we have seen on *CNN* than we are to trust something we read in *News of the World* or heard on the local college radio station. Bloggers build trust individually. Some of the strategies are the same as for mainstream media – for instance, a blog with professional-looking design may be more likely to convince us than a gaudy blog that looks as though it was designed by an amateur. There are countless exceptions to this, however. If Salam Pax's blog had looked overly designed, we might not have trusted it as an authentic example of an ordinary Baghdad citizen's blog. We trust or distrust bloggers on the basis of our perception of their honesty.

This kind of personal authenticity can be faked, of course, but fakes tend to be found out in the blogosphere. Bloggers are an inquisitive species. Although some blogs that fake authenticity have had success for a while, they have suffered hefty negative backlashes when exposed as fakes. You can read about some examples of this in chapter 6 on commercial blogging, which is the field where the temptation to create fake blogging personas is the strongest.

It should also be noted that authenticity doesn't necessarily require complete self-exposure. Many bloggers, even news bloggers and political bloggers, use pseudonyms. If a blogger becomes popular enough or controversial enough, readers will likely try to figure out the blogger's real identity. When the Iraqi blogger Salam Pax became read by thousands during the US invasion of Iraq, there were lively debates as to whether he was authentic. Could Salam Pax really be an Iraqi living in Baghdad, or was he a fake? Was his blog propaganda from Saddam Hussein's government, trying to make us feel sympathetic towards the Iraqi population? Or was it propaganda from the Americans? In fact, debaters never decided on whose side Salam Pax stood, and perhaps this is the most important point about this kind of direct message from a civilian in a war zone. At some level, it doesn't matter whether the blog is 'real' or 'true' or 'authentic'. It doesn't matter whether the videos of crying children and anxious mothers were *really* posted to YouTube by teenagers in Beirut as Israel dropped bombs on their city. We have already heard the news of the bombings of Beirut and the attacks on Baghdad from mainstream media outlets. The primary function of these blogs and videos is not to be a factual report or confirmation of what is happening. They are highly subjective, emotional reports on events that we already know are happening. Baghdad was being invaded as Salam Pax blogged. And really, all the Lebanese teenagers or Salam Pax were telling us were things we could have imagined for ourselves – but we still wanted to read or see them from people actually experiencing the events. In this sense, the truth of blogs may have more in common with the truth of novels, art and poetry than with the facts presented by journalism.

Classic journalism, Melissa Wall argues, is closely tied to modernity. Wall writes: 'The values that anchored modernity were reflected in journalism: a sense that reality could be observed and documented from an objective viewpoint, an emphasis on constant change and timeliness, and a belief in being able to represent reality accurately' (2005, 154). The profession of journalism and our idea of 'news' developed as recently as the nineteenth century, becoming a commodity that could be sold and resold. During the twentieth century, journalism further developed in order to reach the largest number of people. One strategy was that of presenting the news as objective: 'In order to reach the largest audiences, news was presented as the mere reflection of reality, a detached, neutral report that usually included a counter point of view to any controversy so as to offend the fewest people possible' (155). In reducing discussions to two binary points of view, alternative perspectives would often disappear.

Melissa Wall argues that the group of war blogs she looked at – that is, blogs that discussed the Iraq war – present post-modern characteristics, rather than 'traditional journalism's modern approach'. The postmodern characteristics Wall

identifies are personalization, audience participation in content creation, and story forms that are fragmented and inter-
dependent with other Web sites.

The traditional, modernist form of journalism is today augmented by many other journalistic genres that are subjective
in various ways. Journalists are increasingly presenting themselves as participants in events rather than assuming they can
stay outside. The reporting of politics, wars and crimes is, however, still generally kept in the objective code. For bloggers,
who generally do not aspire to being journalists, trying to stay
objective is completely irrelevant. This may be most apparent
in the first group of blogs that approach journalism: the first-
hand reports. We'll look at two rather different ways in which
bloggers may end up publishing first-hand reports.

First-hand Reports: Blogging from a War Zone

In 2003, at the start of the Iraq war, blogger Salam Pax wrote
almost daily of his life in Baghdad. The details he noted were of
the sort that might be noted by a professional feature journalist, but the experience of hearing directly from a person who
was there, involved in this horrible conflict, made reading the
blog a far stronger experience than reading even an excellent
article by a professional could be. Here are extracts from a post
Salam Pax published on 21 March 2003:

> We got two phone calls from abroad . . . around 6:30 my
> uncle went out to get bread . . . the Iraqi TV was showing
> patriotic songs and didn't even bother to inform viewers that
> we are under attack . . . The Iraqi Satellite Channel is not
> broadcasting anymore. The second youth TV channel (it
> shows Egyptian soaps in the morning and sports afterwards)
> also stopped transmitting.

You could then move on to one of the blogs written by an
American soldier participating in the war, Lieutenant Smash,
later known as Citizen Smash and then as Mr Smash. His
writing was far sparser than Salam Pax's. Here's an extract

from his post on 23 March 2003: 'Still working about 13–14 hours every day. Haven't had a break since Christmas. . . . Reports of deaths and casualties bring mixed emotions. Sadness at the injury or loss of fellow warriors. Relief at the low numbers reported. Hope this ends quickly. But things might get sticky as we close in on the prize.' The tense prose in many ways fits the role a soldier is expected to take: there is some manly grief, perhaps, but one needs to get on with the business at hand. Salam Pax, on the other hand, has time to worry and to write.

Salam Pax's and Lieutenant Smash's blogs are diary-style blogs – they write about what happens to them on a day-to-day basis, and share thoughts on their immediate situation. Their diaries have political importance because of the significant global events they have been thrust into, one as a soldier and the other as a civilian. Their diaries have many similarities to other diaries written by people in a war zone, and such diaries have often been seen as very important documents in our understanding of wars. However, before the Internet made it possible to share a diary in real time with a potentially global audience, wartime diaries were generally not read until after the conflict was over. Anne Frank's diary was retrieved by her father after the war was over and she was dead, and only then was it published. Soldiers have sent letters home, but, though some of these were published while conflict was still taking place, there were no large-scale and immediate publication channels during previous wars, as there are today.

When Salam Pax and Lieutenant Smash began blogging from a war zone they were among the first bloggers to do so – and they were certainly the first to be as widely read and publicized as they were. Salam Pax, especially, became extremely popular as his site was written about in blogs and mainstream media all around the world. Although it is difficult to find exact readership figures, *Wired* (8 May 2003) and other media reported that his blog, which was hosted at blogspot.com, was so overloaded by visitors that both Blogger and Google created mirror sites that readers could visit instead. A few weeks after his blog gained such fame, the *Guardian* recruited Salam Pax as a columnist, and by the end of 2003 much of his blog had been published in book form as *The Baghdad Blog*, first in English by Atlantic Books and then in multiple translations. So in many ways the blog was tamed by mass media as Salam Pax's communication with the world was channelled into the traditional forms of mass distribution that have been honed so well through the twentieth century: newspapers and mass market paperbacks with agents arranging translations and distribution around the world. As such, one could see Salam Pax's blog as having been simply a means for him to be discovered by and recruited into the mainstream media. But although his words probably reached a different demographic through the books and the newspaper columns than they had reached through his blog, the people who only encountered him in mainstream media had a different relationship with him: a different degree of access. The immediate way in which Salam Pax's diary was originally shared with readers across the world led to a community of readers who eagerly discussed his every post and who worried about his well-being, thankful every time a new post was published to show he was still alive.

Salam Pax continued blogging until April 2004, when he left a brief post announcing a hiatus. Four months later he posted a final post consisting simply of a full stop. There have been no more posts to the blog, although he has posted to other temporary blogs and continued to work as a journalist for international media.

At the time of writing, Citizen Smash hasn't added anything to his blog in several months, and the most recent posts on his blog are re-posts of entries published while he was in Iraq. In a close reading of Smash's blog, Michael Keren argues that there was a shift from his early narratives of his experience as a civilian thrust into the life of a soldier to a kind of blogging that largely replicated the official doctrine of the US government and the standardized portrayal of war in movies and other media (Keren 2006, 93–102). For instance, he went from mentioning that he wasn't interested in attending an official Memorial Day service to posting a very traditionally patriotic message on Independence Day, and his last entry on his war experience very closely mirrors the images of soldiers return- ing home in movies and novels.

First-hand Reports: Chance Witnesses

Salam Pax and Lieutenant Smash chose to blog in order to tell the stories of living through a war, as a civilian or as a soldier. They were entirely aware that their blogs would be read by many people. They were emotionally beleaguered, certainly, but were blogging with full knowledge and, it seems, a wish to share their feelings.

A very different dynamics can occur when a blogger who has mostly been writing for close friends and family is suddenly thrust into the limelight because he or she has witnessed and blogged about a major current event. One of the clearest recent examples was seen in the aftermath of the Virginia Tech shoot- ings on 16 April 2007. Statistically, students are among the most likely demographic to blog, so it was no surprise to find that many of the students on campus blogged about the hor- rors of that day. One blogger, who used the alias ntcoolfool for his LiveJournal diary, posted the following few lines at 12:10 pm, just hours after the shootings:

> THE FIRST SHOOTING TOOK PLACE AT AROUND 7AM.
> I WENT TO CLASS AT 9AM. THEY DIDN'T CLOSE
> CAMPUS UNTIL 10AM.
>
> Just like that. We topped Columbine.
>
> Please God, have none of them be my friends. Please.

These words are moving precisely because their author is a participant in the events, and because they are so immediate: we can read them seconds after the blogger typed them and pressed the 'post' button. Ntcoolfool posted fast and often on this day, with separate posts at 10:48 am, 11:45 am, 12:29 am, 2 pm and 4:51 pm, and updates to the final post coming at 5:02 pm, 5:28 pm and 5.50 pm.

A journalist is presumed to be outside of the action, and to observe impartially and objectively. Ntcoolfool is anything but an external observer. He was, admittedly, one step removed, as he was not present in the actual classrooms where the shooting occurred, but his anger, horror and fear for his friends is that of a person directly involved in the event and has none of the distance that traditional journalism aspires to.

Blogs and mainstream media are in many ways symbiotic. The sites blogs link to the most frequently are large mainstream media, although they refer more to blogs in total if you look at the entire list of links (Sifry 2007). Likewise, mainstream media frequently turn to blogs – and on the day of the Virginia Tech shootings, the media quickly found ntcoolfool's LiveJournal and started leaving comments asking him to call them. The first comment on a post that ends 'My friends could be dead. Tears continue' is from a journalist with CBC Newsworld who writes: 'Hi This is [journalist's name] from CBC Newsworld. We are looking for witnesses right now for live phone interviews. Please call me [phone number] ASAP THANKS!' The next comments are from readers complaining at the crassness of the journalist's advance, but this doesn't deter other journalists from posting similar comments on the same post. Ntcoolfool himself doesn't directly respond to this discussion in his blog, but an update to his 4:51 pm post clearly expresses the dilemma that a chance bystander to an event can experience on having their blog suddenly become the centre of global media attention:

UPDATE (5:50):
This is ridiculous. I find myself getting excited because I'm on the news (Fox News recently shared the blog). Each time I hear something else I get a brief moment of selfish joy before I am stabbed in the heart, realizing that I deserve no credit and that lives are gone, destroyed, and in pain. What is the

significance of all this? My postings are simply what I always do – except I left my thoughts for the public instead of just my friends. This run of emotions is hard to bear. I need to go for a walk – but of course, what good is that since everything is outside my door. There is no escaping. The chains have been tied to the door.

Interestingly enough, another site where students at Virginia Tech shared their feelings and experiences was Facebook. As discussed in chapter 3, Facebook is a social networking site that allows conventional blogging, photo sharing, chatting and other kinds of communication, but the default is that this information is only visible to other users you have either named as your 'friend' or who are part of the same network as you, where a network is defined by people who are attending the same school, live in the same place or work with the same company. Because of this limited viewing, the discussion of the Virginia Tech shootings on Facebook was a far more local affair than ntcoolfool's blog. News crews couldn't easily gain access to blog posts and other media shared on Facebook because access was limited to other students at Virginia Tech. On LiveJournal, ntcoolfool could have chosen to make his posts about the shootings private or visible only to his friends, but he explicitly chose to make them public, wanting to share his thoughts with more people. He also appears to have handled his brief media fame quite well, based on other posts he made that day. However, the intensity of suddenly being thrust into extreme media attention can be very straining on a blogger who is used to having a small and intimate audience, and journalists should be very aware of the ethical issues of approaching bloggers who are in crisis, as ntcoolfool was on that day. As the comments from other readers of ntcoolfool's blog show, bloggers and their readers are quick to see journalists as exploitative, in contrast to regular readers, who see themselves as supportive. This is in part because of the rift between the two separate spheres (a rift discussed below in chapter 5, in relation to the *lonelygirl15* videos on YouTube).

Likewise, bloggers should be very aware that, when they blog, what they publish may become a great deal more widespread than they had imagined. This can of course be extremely empowering, but also, sometimes, very difficult to deal with.

Salam Pax, Lieutenant Smash and ntcoolfool are all examples of bloggers who were direct participants in events that were seen as extremely newsworthy by mainstream media and that the general public was hungry to know more about. As participants, they made no attempt to be objective. The traditional journalistic creeds of credibility and fact-checking were of no relevance to them. Their strength was instead their authenticity – but it is a different kind of authenticity from the promise that 'this is true', given by mainstream media. This authenticity is evidenced by the immediacy of the bloggers.

Bloggers as Independent Journalists and Opinionists

The second way that blogs approach journalism is when bloggers more deliberately set out to tell stories that might also be told by journalists.

Christopher Allbritton was a freelance journalist who had spent some time in Iraq before the 2003 invasion. In March 2003, he asked the readers of his blog, back-to-iraq.com, to fund a return trip to Iraq, promising that, in return for donations, he would give readers frequent updates on his trip and genuine news from an independent journalist on the spot. The idea of having an independent journalist in Iraq was appealing at a time when mainstream media was 'embedding' journalists in the US army, which allowed greater insights into army working but also made it harder for the public to see the reports coming from these journalists as unbiased. But the greatest attraction of Allbritton's plan to travel to Iraq as a journalist directly funded by his readers was the promise of direct communication. In the months leading up to the project, Allbritton spent a lot of time on his blog, writing carefully researched articles and responding directly to reader questions. Readers who donated to his trip were placed on an email list where they received his reports from the field several hours earlier than regular blog readers who had not contributed money, and readers were also encouraged to submit comments and to suggest topics they'd like Allbritton to cover. Allbritton succeeded in raising US $15,000, enough to fund his trip, although his visit only lasted a few weeks due to security issues. He returned to Baghdad in May 2004, but again the expenses of maintaining basic security, paying a driver and so on led him to work as a conventional freelance journalist for the mainstream media instead of continuing as an independent journalist. Despite the apparent untenability of independent reader-funded journalism in a war zone, the experiment was successful to a point, and it's possible that similar strategies will be developed further in the future.

Another conventionally newsworthy subject is politics, and there are many bloggers who write extensively about politics – as noted in chapter 1, in the 2006 Pew Internet survey on bloggers, 11 per cent of the bloggers interviewed stated that their main topic is politics (Lenhart and Fox 2006). Most of these bloggers link to and comment on information published in the mainstream media or directly on politicians' Web sites and campaign Web sites. They may focus on being watchdogs, tracking everything done by or written about a particular candidate or issue. Frequently their posts will take the form of opinion pieces or contributions to a debate – either among bloggers or in the public at large.

Some of these bloggers have gone to great efforts to obtain direct access to political events. The US Democratic Convention in 2004 was a breakthrough for bloggers wanting press access, as three dozen bloggers were given press credentials to the convention (*New York Times*, 26 July 2004). Since then, bloggers with well-established and serious blogs have frequently gained press access to similar events.

Gatewatching

The third way in which journalism and blogging intersect is through a practice that Axel Bruns calls gatewatching (Bruns 2005). Gatewatching is a term that plays upon the idea of gatekeeping in traditional media. 'At its most basic', Bruns writes, 'gatekeeping simply refers to a regime of control over what content is allowed to emerge from the production processes in print and broadcast media; the controllers (journalists, editors, owners) of these media, in other words, control the gates through which content is released to their audiences' (2005, 11). There are three different 'gates' or stages involved in this gatekeeping, and each gate contributes to keeping traditional journalism a closed process. First, there is the input phase, where news is gathered – but it is only gathered by staff journalists. Second, there is the output stage, where news is published – but there is a closed editorial hierarchy that restricts what will be published. Third, there is the response stage, where readers comment on the news – but there is an editorial selection of which letters or responses will be made public.

This closed system is collapsing in today's world of participatory media, and we are seeing alternative systems cropping up instead, such as gatewatching. Bruns defines gatewatching as 'the observation of the output gates of news publications and other sources, in order to identify important material as it becomes available' (2005, 17). This kind of observation frequently happens in open news sites or collaborative blogs where readers submit stories they have spotted in the media, and a group of editors or a system of collaborative filtering organizes the stories so that some are shown prominently on the site to be shared with everyone. Digg.com is one such site, although only some of the stories shown on the first page of Digg are conventional news stories.

Blogs written by individuals often perform this kind of gatewatching by virtue of their linking to sources:

> This practice of outwardly directed referencing is virtually
> identical to gatewatching, of course (if, where done by indi-
> viduals, largely ad hoc and non-systematic), and we have
> already made a similar argument for the importance of gate-
> watching in collaborative news sites – there, too, the inclu-
> sion of links to primary and additional outside resources
> plays the role both of enabling readers to check the accuracy
> of reports for themselves and of highlighting that in spite of
> any personal opinion which authors of news reports on the
> site may have expressed they have the intellectual honesty
> to open up the news process to outside scrutiny. (Bruns
> 2005, 180–1)

However, while blogs written by individuals do frequently link
to mainstream media, they also tend to link to other bloggers'
commentary on those news stories, and so they are less dominated by this gatewatching function than are larger community sites such as *Slashdot* or *Kuro5hin*.

Slashdot is a popular site that is sometimes referred to as a
blog, though it is a lot more complex than a basic blog. *Slashdot*
is a very large-scale community site, where readers may contribute stories that may then be featured on the front page.
Typically, front-page stories are brief, consisting of a few links
and a few lines of commentary, but the discussions about each
story can reach thousands of entries. *Slashdot* uses a system of
'karma points', where registered users are assigned modera-
tion duties on certain days, and on those days they have a fixed
number of karma points to assign comments. Comments are
rated according to whether or not they add to the discussion,
and according to whether moderators have found them interesting, funny or informative. When you read comments, you
can choose how many comments you wish to see: all of them,
or only the best.

Slashdot filters the news for its user base: self-declared
'nerds' who are interested in technology and programming,
but also in societal implications of technology, such as changes
in copyright law and in notions of privacy. For instance, one
front-page story on *Slashdot* in December 2007 was that of the

convicted rapist who was murdered by a neighbour who had found his name by searching the 'Megan's Law' database of sex offenders and said that he killed the man to protect his child from being molested. The database entry for the murdered man was incorrect – he was indeed a rapist, but of adults, not children. This story is of particular interest to *Slashdot* users because of the questions of privacy that are raised when we can access increasing amounts of information about individuals online.

Slashdotters' discussion of the case ranges from infantile to highly insightful. If you choose to view only the most highly ranked comments, you might read one given the highest mark and scored as 'Insightful'. The user CreatureComfort notes that the murderer was recently released from jail for assault:

> Gee, it sure seems like the guy convicted of assault with a deadly weapon had a much higher recidivism rate. Not to mention that the guy he killed never molested a child, or a male. Maybe we should just have an offender registry that lists everyone who has ever been convicted of any crime? After all, maybe you don't want to buy that house on the same block as the lady who has received 5 speeding tickets . . . your kids wouldn't be safe in the front yard. After all speeders are notoriously recidivist, and the cause of many highway fatalities.

At the other end of the scale is a comment by 'Anonymous Coward', the pseudonym *Slashdot* automatically assigns to anyone who posts a comment without using a user account: 'I hate sex offenders. We need more people like this man who will go out and bring these monsters waht (*sic*) I call old fashioned justice.' This comment has been marked by other users as 'Flamebait' and given the score −1. That means that most users will never see it, and the tag 'Flamebait' warns users that the poster is likely only trying to stir up a fight rather than contribute to a meaningful discussion.

Bruns also considers whether blog indices like Technorati and Daypop, or earlier indices like Blogdex, function as gatewatchers – perhaps, by automatically filtering millions of individual blogs, they can 'identify important material as it becomes available' in a way more powerful than any single blog. These blog indices perform 'a form of automated large-scale gatewatching, well beyond the small-group collaborative blogging of group blogs' (2005, 207). However, Bruns finds that in practice indices such as these have a relatively low degree of gatewatching, because they tend to find 'blog entries which a large majority of other blogs link to – entries which should therefore be expected to contain more original insight than those blog posts which reference them' (2005, 186). This may have changed somewhat in the years since Bruns wrote *Gatewatching*. Technorati now displays lists of the most linked-to videos posted to YouTube as well as the most linked-to blogs, new items and movies. As Bruns notes, we're seeing rapid technological advances in search and content recognition, and as a result large-scale forms of gatewatching that use blogs to see larger trends are likely to develop considerably in years to come.

Bruns' discussion of blogs as potential gatewatchers largely emphasizes the role blogs serve in filtering the news, that is, in determining which news stories readers actually end up seeing. However, the most interesting examples of gatewatching in blogs occur when bloggers act as watchdogs of the media, finding errors or omissions in the reporting conducted by mainstream journalists. In these cases, a feedback loop between blogs and mainstream media is established, where the bloggers use existing news stories to break new news, which then in turn is reported on by the mainstream media.

One of the most famous of these occasions was the so-called 'Rathergate' scandal in 2004. The popular anchor of CBS Evening News, Dan Rather, presented a set of documents that were critical of President George W. Bush's time in the military. Rather announced that the documents were from the 1970s, and that experts at CBS had confirmed them as authentic. Within hours, however, bloggers had begun to question the authenticity of the documents, and began to question the typography, arguing that the font used in the documents did not exist in the 1970s. The story quickly fed back into the mainstream media and ultimately led to Dan Rather being demoted.

Another blogger who dug deeper where mainstream journalists failed is Magnus Ljungkvist. Shortly after the announcement of a new government in Sweden, the mainstream media discovered that Maria Borelius, a newly appointed minister, had several years previously used nannies for her children without paying the taxes she was supposed to pay as an employer. When questioned on this by journalists, Borelius answered that she hadn't been able to afford it at the time, and the journalist took her answer at face value. Ljungkvist was more inquisitive, and searched the minister's tax records – in Sweden, tax records are available for public searching online – and found that her income during the period she had the nanny had been far above the average Swedish income. He published this in his blog and received a lot of attention from other bloggers, and eventually from the mainstream media, which followed up on the figures Ljungkvist had found. Shortly thereafter, Borelius resigned as minister, and the following year Ljungkvist was awarded a national award for citizen journalism.

Both the Rathergate and the Ljungkvist/Borelius affairs show how tightly intermingled blogging and mainstream journalism can be. Blogging and journalism are often seen as being in opposition to each other, and both stories can be told to show that the bloggers 'won' over traditional journalism. However, it is equally clear that in both stories there is an interaction between the traditional and the unruly.

Ljungkvist and the Rathergate bloggers were gatewatchers, in Axel Bruns' terms, although they went a step further than simply watching and republishing the news. Bloggers like these follow mainstream media closely, and when mainstream media slips up and makes a mistake, they pounce on it, do their own independent research and publish their version of the story. They can do this because ordinary citizens today have an unprecedented ability to do such research – we have easy access to many databases and archives that would have been inaccessible to ordinary citizens only ten or fifteen years ago. In addition, bloggers have access to community. If an issue generates interest in the blogosphere, many minds can think together in ways that can be extremely powerful, as the Rathergate case shows.

Symbiosis

Much of the literature on blogs is enthusiastic about the ways in which blogs empower ordinary citizens who previously have not had access to the media or to the public sphere. There is no doubt that blogs have allowed people to share ideas and build resistance in non-democratic countries such as China and Iran, where censorship is heavy but blogs are able to slip through. Blogs allowed us to read the thoughts of a young man in Baghdad during the invasion of Iraq, or to read the immedi-ate response of another young man whose classmates were shot at Virginia Tech – and this immediate connection with people in the middle of globally reported events appears to bring us closer together. Bloggers have seen themselves as an alternative to mainstream media, and as a force that can reform and change the ways we conceive of media: today, any-body can own a press. Anybody can be the media.

However, blogs and social media serve the purposes of mainstream media as well. The mainstream media were quick to republish blog posts written by the young man at Virginia Tech, and to interview him. The mainstream media recruited Salam Pax to write newspaper columns. Some newspapers offer free blog hosting and use the best posts as free content for the newspaper. They ask readers and viewers who have been present at newsworthy events to send in photos, videos and reports that are then integrated into the mainstream news story. Many journalists keep their own blogs. One such journalist, J. D. Lasica, writes that 'many journalists who blog are doing just that – exposing the raw material of their stories-in-progress, asking readers for expert input, posting complete text of interviews alongside the published story, and writing follow-up stories based on outsiders' tips and suggestions' (Lasica 2003).

Another way in which blogs can be said to support mainstream media has been expressed by Geert Lovink: 'Blogs test. They allow you to see whether your audience is still awake and receptive. In that sense we could also say that blogs are the outsourced, privatized test beds, or rather unit tests of the big media' (Lovink 2007a). This argument is perhaps most useful insofar as it inverts the common utopian argument that blogs empower readers and viewers, allowing us to create media instead of simply consuming them. Lovink asserts the opposite: that blogs are the servants of the mainstream media, simply providing a more nuanced form of audience survey at no cost to the media. Trying to think of blogs as nothing more than this allows us also to see the absurdity of thinking of blogs as nothing but citizen journalism, empowering the bloggers. Bloggers may be amateurs, but in many cases that is a benefit, not a disadvantage: 'Blog space gives amateurs a way to enter the debate – "amateur" not in the sense of inexperienced, but in the sense of an Olympic athlete, meaning not paid by anyone to give their reports' (Lessig 2004, 44).

Yochai Benkler, in his influential book *The Wealth of Networks*, notes that, while professional journalists working for mainstream media appear to have a great many advantages in comparison to bloggers, bloggers have their own advantages:

> [C]learly the unorganized collection of Internet users lacks some of the basic tools of the mass media: dedicated full-time reporters; contacts with politicians who need media to survive, and therefore cannot always afford to stonewall questions; or public visibility and credibility to back their

assertions. However, network-based peer production also avoids the inherent conflicts between investigative reporting and the bottom line – its cost, its risk of litigation, its risk of withdrawal of advertising from alienated corporate subjects, and its risk of alienating readers. (Benkler 2006, 264–5)

Obviously, blogs are many different things. What appears to be clear, however, is that blogs need mainstream media, and that, today, the mainstream media also need blogs.

CHAPTER FIVE

Blogs as Narratives

In this chapter, I'll examine blogging as a form of narrative and as a form of self-representation. The format of blogs means that narratives – whether fictional or authentic – are structured in certain ways that are different from the ways narratives are organized in movies or novels. Blogs that primarily tell the story of a life or lives, as confessional blogs do, also come with problems of their own, as when readers discover that a blog they have treated as the sincere narrative of a real person's experience is actually a fiction.

Blogging is an episodic style of writing that leads to particular kinds of narrative structure. Both diaries and earlier hypertext fiction are antecedents of this narrative structure, and I'll look at connections between blogging and both these forms of narrative. Most blogging is to some extent self-representational, and as such a form of life-writing or autobiography. But sometimes blogs that are written as though they are authentic turn out to be fictional. When this happens, readers often respond with fury and outrage. We'll look at two examples of this, the Kaycee Nicole case, and that of *lonelygirl15*, a videoblogger who posted her videos to YouTube.

Fragmented Narratives

The most obvious difference between narrative in a blog and in a novel is that the stories in blogs are told in brief episodes. Each post in a blog has a beginning and an end, and can in principle be read on its own. Read together, the posts create a larger story.

Episodic narrative is an established format that we know from soap operas, television serials, comic books and serially published fiction. However, the cliffhangers we're familiar with from these genres, with the excitement of the 'to be continued' coming in the middle of action, do not generally occur with blogs. Each blog post is far briefer than are most episodes of these other kinds of serial narratives, and there is not always a clear sense of continuity between posts as there is in a serial.

Another antecedent of this fragmented kind of narrative is hypertext fiction, a literary form that began to develop in the late 1980s, when the first hypertext authoring tools, such as Apple's HyperCard and Eastgate System's StorySpace, became readily available (Bolter 2001, Douglas 2000, Hayles 2007). Michael Joyce's *afternoon, a story* (1990) is generally recognized as the first hypertext fiction, and, like a blog, it consists of many small pieces of narrative, called nodes or lexias, which are connected by links. *Afternoon* is still very unlike a blog, because when the reader first encounters the work it is already clear that this is a finished product. Because *afternoon* was written before the existence of the Web, the work was published as a stand-alone piece of software, bought on a diskette. The reader may never read the whole work, and may in fact be frustrated in trying to read the whole work, but still knows that it is there, potentially accessible. The reader of a blog, on the other hand, cannot know when or even whether a blog will end, and, even when a blog does end, questions are not necessarily resolved for the reader.

During the 1990s, hypertext fiction moved online (Walker 2005b), and some of these Web-based hypertexts made use of the infinite extendibility of the Web. *The Unknown* (Gillespie, Rettberg, Stratton and Marquardt 1998) is a good example of this: this hypertext novel is narrated by fictional characters who bear the same names as the actual authors of the work. The story is about the four protagonists' long-lasting book tour, and consists of hundreds of densely interlinked nodes that were written over the course of several years. In *The Unknown*, the dramatic arc is more similar to that of a blog than to a traditional novel. The story is told in interlinked fragments, and the reader wanders through the narrative without knowing when it will end. However, pages are not dated, and the reader has no information about which pages were written first or last.

Goal-oriented Narrative

Some blogs do have a very clear dramatic arc, as when a blogger starts a blog with a clear project in mind. One amusing example of such a blog was *The Date Project*, a blog set up by a young man who was determined to find a girlfriend. On 4 June 2002, in his second post, he set himself three rules:

> One: I will strike up a conversation with three different people I do not know each day.
>
> Two: I will attend activities, events, or other situations where I can meet new people at least twice a week.
>
> Three: I will ask out at least one woman each week.

The blogger, who simply called himself 'Anonymous', blogged his progress as a way of keeping himself accountable. However, on day two of his project, a friend set him up on a blind date with 'K', and by day twenty-seven Anonymous shut down *The Date Project* with the following words: 'It's over. I am in love, "K" and I are happy, and life goes on.'

While this is of course a highly successful project for the anonymous blogger, as journalist John Hiler notes, it is not a particularly satisfying narrative for us readers:

> I'm realizing that the whole fun of dating blogs comes from vicariously experiencing the frustrations and humiliations of the dating circuit. It's no fun when someone finds true love in, say . . . twenty-seven days (?!). It's like Bridget Jones getting married in the first chapter, or Carrie Bradshaw meeting

Mr. Big in the first season (oh wait, that one did happen).
(Hiler 2002)

Happiness, of course, is 'the death knell for any dating blog', as
Hiler wryly remarks.

The narrative structure of a blog like *The Date Project* is
always projected forwards. There is a goal that is clearly
expressed when the blog is started, and that is often even sum-
marized in the sidebar for new readers. The blog will end when
– or if – the goal is achieved. Dating blogs aren't the only kind
of blog that set up this kind of project. A presumably fictional
blog called *She's a Flight Risk* used the premise of a very wealthy
heiress who had run away from home to avoid a marriage she
didn't want. The blog is no longer at its original URL, but if you
look it up in archive.org, the wonderful site that archives large
chunks of the Internet, you'll find that the sidebar of the blog
announced the premise in brief: 'On March 2, 2003 at 4:12
pm, I disappeared. My name is isabella v., but it's not. I'm
twentysomething and I am an international fugitive.' Here a
clear starting point is defined with a clear goal: to escape her
father. At the same time, this is a narrative premise that suits
blogs because of its emphasis on process – running away –
rather than on a short-term goal.

Dieting blogs are another kind of blog that use this format.
A clear goal is set, and the public diary is used to keep the
dieter accountable. Yet there is a flexibility in this form of diary,
as well, as Diane Greco noted in her blog, *Narcissism, vanity,
exhibitionism, ambition, vanity, vanity, vanity*, on 25 February
2004:

> By and large, the blogs tell success stories. They have to –
> blogging as a literary form supports the idea of eventual suc-
> cess. When there's bad news from the bathroom scale, the
> open-endedness of blogging makes it possible to cast the gain
> as just a temporary setback, not a failure. Diet blogging
> recasts or reimagines the yo-yo effects of a diet as a surface, a
> space, a site for potentially endless re-inscription. Dieting as
> Etch-a-Sketch, very postmodern.

Ongoing Narration

In his dissection of narrative desire, Peter Brooks writes of the '*anticipation of retrospection* as our chief tool in making sense of narrative' (Brooks 1984, 23). We read with a certainty that there will *be* an end and that, when we have reached it, we will be able to look back and see the whole.

When blogs tell stories, they generally do so in an episodic form, with each post being a self-contained unit that contributes to an overall narrative. Each post makes sense in itself, but read together – not necessarily in sequence – the posts tell a larger story. That story is usually partial and incomplete, and does not form a narrative whole as well-formed stories in mainstream literature and cinema do. Instead, the overall story as gleaned from reading a blog is likely to be pieced together from fragments, perhaps supplemented by bits of stories from other places.

In chapter 2 we looked at Jason Kottke's blog, Kottke.org. His blog, along with *MegNut*, the blog of his wife, Meg Hourihan, shows how such an overall story can be pieced together by a regular reader. The development of Kottke's and Hourihan's relationship, as seen through their blogs, is neatly chronicled by Rebecca Mead in a story she wrote for the *New Yorker*. Mead relates how readers heard briefly of Kottke and Hourihan living together in San Francisco before moving to New York together. A year later, readers of *MegNut* and Kottke.org who read between the lines might have pieced together a less rosy picture:

> [W]hen Meg took off for Nantucket in the summer of 2004, the move was conspicuously undertaken in the first-person singular. In December, 2004, she wrote a post entitled 'A Sad Breakup'; and while its subject was Barbie, whose boyfriend, Ken, had sometime earlier been sidelined by Mattel for a new beau, Blaine, attentive readers wondered whether a more significant allusion was being made. . . . Meanwhile, Jason was blogging moodily about hiring a man with a van to move his stuff across town. (Mead 2006)

Things looked better the following year. Although neither Kottke nor Hourihan explicitly mentioned their relationship, they both mentioned a trip to Ireland at about the same time. In November 2005 Hourihan announced their engagement on her blog, and the following March she posted their wedding photo. Since then, they have become parents. There was little mention of the pregnancy on their blogs, but a few days after the baby was born both Kottke and Hourihan posted photographs of their son on their blogs, along with brief announcements. The baby hasn't since been the main focus of their blog posts, but does show up in their blogs occasionally. For instance, Hourihan, who since changing professions from technology to cooking mainly blogs about food, published a post about eating during pregnancy a little later, while Kottke, as we saw in chapter 1, jokingly compared the baby's reflexes to the accelerometres of new electronic gadgets.

Bloggers often avoid writing directly about their emotional and personal affairs. Neither Hourihan nor Kottke write confessional or diary-style blogs. Their blogs are filter blogs with specific topics: technology and design for Kottke, and food and cooking for Hourihan, though her blog used to be focused on Web technology. They didn't blog that they had broken up – but observant readers might piece together the pieces if they followed the blogs over a long period of time.

Episodic narratives are particularly well suited to our style of reading on the Internet. Usability guru Jakob Nielsen has notoriously pointed out that users *don't* read on the Web, they scan and skim (Nielsen 1997). Although it has become a commonplace to claim that 'I hate reading on a screen', we're certainly spending more and more time with texts on screens. Emails, online newspapers, weblogs, online shopping, Facebook and other familiar screen texts don't usually follow Nielsen's 1997 rules for bullet lists and bold keywords, but they do provide reasonably brief nuggets of text that each make some sense on their own. We may not be happy reading 500-page blockbusters on our computer screens (though a really *good* ebook reader might change that), but we spend hours reading and moving between fragments.

Weblogs are an obvious example of the success of serial narrative on the Web. Most posts in weblogs are short enough to be read in a few minutes. Instead of watching a twenty-two-minute episode of a television serial each week, a weblog is read in two- or five-minute sessions once a day or once every few days or at irregular intervals. Added up, regular readers of a weblog spend a considerable number of hours perusing their favourite blog over the years.

Justin Hall's blog *Justin's Links* is a far more deliberate narration of the blogger's life than are the blogs of Jason Kottke and Meg Hourihan. Hall is a pioneer of online journaling, and began writing his life online in 1994 (Hall 2004). As Rob Wittig relates in a review of *Justin's Links*, the temporality of the site was always a major narrative hook:

> I'll never forget the Monday morning in the mid-90s when I rushed in to work (my only Internet connection at the time, imagine!) and hurriedly pointed my browser to www.links.net to see if Justin Hall had broken up with his girlfriend over the weekend. I didn't know Justin personally. Still don't. But I had been enjoying his groundbreaking Web diary for several months, had turned some co-workers on to it, and all of us had gotten swept up in Justin's inner (and quite public) turmoil as The Big Conversation loomed. (Wittig 2003)

Wittig continues by noting how, when he returns to reading *Justin's Links* years later, the freshest posts have elisions that whet his curiosity, pushing him to read more in order to fill in the holes in the narrative as best as he can. Justin writes:

> Riding the 11.10pm bus from Tokyo into the country-side the navel of Japan Gifu that's both hotter in the summer and colder in the winter, where we will gladly step off at 5am in the country where we might have her mom take care of us some, meaning we'll have only family things to worry about, as the rest of life will be limited to 33k slow bauds through expensive everywhere slow wireless japan. (links.net, 14 November 2002)

Wittig asks, hungry for more: 'Who is the new "her" of "her mom?" How long has he been in Japan? I must read on!' One of the main fascinations of this kind of narration is that the narrative moves in the same time frame as that within which our own lives play out.

This is a different brand of narrative desire to the kind Peter Brooks argued was triggered by novels. While Brooks discussed the novel reader's desire to reach the end, a blog reader's desire is instead always for the next post. The blog reader hopes that there is no end. An end would not tie up all the loose ends, answer the questions and make the narrative into a neat, comprehensible whole. It would simply be a stop. As Phillippe Lejeune writes of diaries, 'All journal writing assumes the intention to write at least one more time, an entry that will call for yet another one, and so on without end. . . . To "finish" a diary means to cut it off from the future' (Lejeune 2001, 100–1).

Most blogs end when their writers simply stop writing. Sometimes this is explained. Some blogs were set up for a specific project, such as losing weight (*Tales of a Bathroom Scale*), having a baby in the face of infertility (*A Little Pregnant*), finding a girlfriend (*The Date Project*) or paying off debts (*We're in Debt*). When the goal is achieved, the blog often ends. Sometimes the blogger feels that they have developed a persona in the blog that traps them, not allowing them to write as they now want to write. Dr Crazy's blog, *Chronicles of Dr. Crazy*, was an example of this. For a semester, the blogger who called herself Dr Crazy wrote primarily about life as a young, single academic who wants to have a sex life and still retain academic respect. After some time, she posted a final post to her blog, writing:

> For a long time now, I've felt somewhat hemmed in by the space that I designed in the blogosphere. The pseudonym that was supposed to give me freedom in fact limited me: because of the voice that I had chosen for 'Dr. Crazy,' and because of some of the things that I had chosen to write, I felt

like I had to be very careful about what I revealed about my work. I had aimed, in the beginning, to compose a blog that allowed me to look at the personal and the professional in conjunction, but that was not what I'd achieved. What I'd achieved was the construction of a space, identity, and voice, that allowed for me to talk about personal life things but that ultimately stripped me of all authority (and of all ability to defend my positions) about the professional. (*Chronicles of Dr. Crazy*, 4 January 2006)

This blogger chose to quit publishing *Chronicles of Dr. Crazy* and instead start a new blog, where she could establish a new voice allowing her to write differently.

Sometimes an event leads a blogger to quit. Justin Hall, one of the most prolific personal bloggers ever, put a stop to his personal blog, Links.net, by posting a tearfully emotional ten-minute video in January 2005 describing his distress about the blog, struggling with his inability to combine his deep need to make media, write, publish, share, with his need to have meaningful relationships and love. In the video, he describes how important blogging is to him, and talks about the dilemma this poses when people he cares about don't want him to write about them: 'Because I can't write about people because they don't want to be there and I have nothing to write about . . . and I publish my life on the fucking Internet and it doesn't make people want to be with me, it makes people not trust me and I don't know what the fuck to do about it' (Hall 2005). Hall didn't delete his blog archives, but hid them so you need to know the URL or to have come via a link or a search engine to find the blog posts. There are no more blog posts after January 2005, although Hall does now maintain a professional blog with no personal details whatsoever.

The most final ending of all is death. When a blogger dies, the blog does not necessarily come to an immediate end. Often, the software allows readers to continue to post comments. Sometimes a relative or friend will post a notice on the blog to tell readers what has happened. Eventually, the blog will probably be deleted when the blogger fails to pay the bill to renew the domain.

Blogs as Self-exploration

Viviane Serfaty characterizes weblogs as simultaneously mirrors and veils (Serfaty 2004). Just as we study ourselves in a mirror, shaping our features so our reflections please us, so we create a reflection of ourselves in a weblog. At the same time, we use our blogs to veil ourselves, not telling all but presenting only certain carefully selected aspects of our selves to our readers.

Pseudonymous blogs often play a flirtatious game of peek-a-boo, showing but not showing all. For instance, the pseudonymous blogger may tell us about funny episodes (this guy I saw at the coffee shop!) or life-altering concerns (shall I have a child?) in a tone of voice as though she were writing to a close friend. Regular readers come to know the characters and places in the blogger's life, and easily forget that there are also myriad experiences and thoughts that the blogger deliberately doesn't share on his or her blog. Often pseudonymous bloggers post photographs to their weblog, cropped only to show themselves from the chin down, or with their eyes blocked out, as if wearing an inverted veil. Pseudonymous blogs often have no links to archives. They exist in the moment, an autobiography of now, yet to regular readers there is a long history and a slow feeling of growing to know the author. That, of course, is largely due to our susceptibility to stories. As Wolfgang Iser pointed out in the seventies, readers are experts at filling in the gaps (*lehrstelle*) in a narrative (Iser 1988).

A pseudonymous blog like *Chronicles of Dr. Crazy* was a clearly personal blog about its author's life and thoughts, and posts regularly appeared that were explicitly for the purpose of thinking through a topic important to the writer. Sometimes she asked for advice or opinions, and commentators were often supportive and helpful. Blogs that stick to discussing topics outside of personal, day-to-day experience can have a similarly self-reflective function, as Rebecca Blood, a pioneer blogger, wrote in an early essay on blogs:

> Shortly after I began producing *Rebecca's Pocket* I noticed two side effects I had not expected. First, I discovered my own interests. I thought I knew what I was interested in, but after linking stories for a few months I could see that I was much more interested in science, archaeology, and issues of injustice than I had realized. More importantly, I began to value more highly my own point of view. In composing my link text every day I carefully considered my own opinions and ideas, and I began to feel that my perspective was unique and important. (Blood 2000)

While we might think that a personal blog such as *Chronicles of Dr. Crazy* gave a more comprehensive picture of the blogger than Rebecca Blood's topic-driven blog, the bloggers' own experience is clearly more complicated than this. Blood describes her blog as being a useful self-reflective tool, allowing her to see sides of herself that she hadn't fully realized the importance of. In this respect, her blog was like the mirror Serfaty refers to. Dr Crazy, on the other hand, finds that the image of herself portrayed in her blog obscures a crucial part of her personality, namely her professional authority. Her blog became a veil that turned out to hide part of what she wanted to explore. When pseudonymous bloggers post photos of themselves that show some of their faces, but not all, or show them but only from behind, they simultaneously use their blogs as mirrors and as veils – exploring themselves, hiding parts of themselves, and looking through the veil, to communicate with their readers.

Fictions or Hoaxes? Kaycee Nicole and *lonelygirl15*

One of the first widely publicized cases of a fake blog or diary was that of Kaycee Nicole, who presented herself as a high-school student who was fighting leukaemia. Kaycee became more and more popular, and developed and maintained friendships not only through her blog, *Living Colours* (since taken offline), but also through email and in chat rooms. In time, Kaycee's mother Debbie started a companion blog about caring for a child with cancer. When Kaycee eventually died in 2001, her online friends were devastated. However, not long after her reported death, some bloggers started seeing inconsistencies in her story, and began wondering whether she might not have been a hoax. Much of the discussion and detective work that led to Kaycee's exposure as a fake is documented in a *Metafilter* discussion thread started on 18 May 2001 (acridrabbit et.al. 2001). When Kaycee's friends found out that both Kaycee and Debbie were fictional, they were furious. They felt deceived and used (Geitgey 2001; Powazek 2001; Woning 2001).

The Kaycee Nicole case was neither the first nor the last time fictional characters have been presented and interpreted as being real. Orson Welles' radio production of H. G. Wells' *War of the Worlds* in 1938 is the most well-known example of widespread belief that a fiction is true. Welles' Halloween joke was taken as fact by thousands of listeners, who panicked, believing that Martians had attacked planet Earth and annihilated much of the United States. Welles had dramatized the science fiction story as though it were being reported live on radio. The play started as though it were a regular radio programme, with introductory piano music. The music was broken off by announcements that abnormal activities had been observed on Mars, and then that Martian troops had landed in New Jersey. The play became more and more dramatic, with the radio reporter instructing listeners to seek open spaces and avoid congested areas, and culminated in a description of gigantic Martians striding across the Hudson River and demolishing New York. By this point, many listeners had already fled their homes and did not hear the ad break that followed the fictional death of the announcer in New York. According to one survey, as many as 28 per cent of listeners believed that the play had been a real news report (Cantril, Gaudet and Herzog 1966).

Both *War of the Worlds* and Kaycee Nicole mimicked media genres that were fairly new at the time, that of radio broadcast and that of confessional blogs. Neither genre is used predominantly for fiction, in fact, most radio broadcasts are explicitly factual and most blogs are sincere reports of an actual individual's ideas or experiences. Most of the fiction we encounter is clearly delimited – a novel is enclosed between the two covers of a book and is clearly labelled as a novel. Movies are watched with a set of rituals around them clearly telling us what is part of the fictional movie and what is not. We usually watch movies in a cinema or using the full screen of a television or computer. Additionally, movies use title sequences and end credits much as novels use covers, title pages and tables of contents: to show us what is part of the fiction and what is not. In new genres such as radio in the 1930s and blogs at the turn of the twenty-first century, such conventions were not established. In the case of blogs, they may never be established, as the Web does not present closed, whole works in the same way as books, movies and even television with its clear schedules tend to. The Web is not part of the Gutenberg parenthesis that we discussed in chapter 2. On the Web, we read in fragments – maybe we spend five minutes a day checking a favourite blog, wander around looking at YouTube videos for twenty minutes, read some email and then follow a link to a Web site a friend recommended. This means that fiction is not always clearly marked as such. Or even if it is, we might not see those signposts, because we haven't read the entire diary or seen all the videos in the YouTube channel.

While Orson Welles and his Mercury Theatre on the Air created *War of the Worlds* as fiction and as art and entertainment, the anonymous woman who created Kaycee had no obvious motive. She did not make any money out of the elaborate fiction. On the contrary: she sent generous presents to many of her – or rather Kaycee's – online friends. Kaycee's creator put a lot of time and care into building and maintaining relationships with her readers. She poured emotions into the role she acted, crying on the phone to van der Woning, for instance, when she was playing the role of Kaycee's mother Debbie (Woning 2001). For the actual woman who performed as Kaycee, Kaycee was fictional. She constructed and found a set of objects that she used as props in her own game of make-believe: photos of the girl next door, various Web sites, presents. Kaycee's name, personality, age and the nature of her illness were basic tenets that determined what was possible within this fictional world.

A more recent fictional blog that also received a lot of publicity was the video blog *lonelygirl15*. Lonelygirl15 was the user name of a 16 year old girl, Bree, who posted video blog entries to YouTube every few days during the summer of 2006. At first her videos seemed unremarkable, much like the many other video diaries kept by teenage girls on YouTube, but, as time went on, her story became stranger and stranger. She was home-schooled, and her parents were very restrictive. More ominously, her family were members of some kind of a sect or cult, and Bree had been chosen to take a prominent part in some ritual they were planning. This involved a lot of preparation on Bree's part, including strange dietary requirements and learning an ancient language. Bree had a good friend, Daniel, who also posted videos to YouTube, and both Bree and Daniel actively took part in the YouTube community, participating in discussions in their comment sections and mentioning other popular YouTubers. Bree also had her own MySpace profile, and exchanged emails with fans and friends from YouTube. By the end of the summer, *lonelygirl15* was one of the most subscribed-to channels on YouTube.

But in September 2006, after much speculation among her fans, *lonelygirl15* was revealed to be a hoax, a carefully scripted narrative created by screenwriters and filmmakers Ramesh Flinders and Miles Beckett. Bree was not, in fact, a 16 year old girl, but was played by the actress Jessica Rose. Daniel was likewise played by an actor, and Bree's emails and comments were written by Amanda Solomon Goodfried, a supervising producer and supporting actor in the series (Heffernan 2006).

In contrast to the case of Kaycee Nicole, *lonelygirl15* was designed as a fiction from the start, and the characters in the videos were hired actors. However, the videos were not explicitly announced as fictional, and it was not until viewers revealed that the story was not true that the creators came forward and admitted that they had created *lonelygirl15* as an experiment in new forms of cinematic storytelling. After being exposed, they continued to produce the series, though now explicitly as a fiction. They have experimented with various ways of making money from this kind of online fiction, such as product placements, and there have been spin-offs, such as an Alternative Reality Game based on the series. The creators also embarked on a new series, *Kate Modern*, which uses similar narrative techniques but is integrated into the British social networking site Bebo.com. This time they're being upfront about the project's fictional nature – and they're also deliberately planning advertising and other ways to make a profit from their endeavour.

When Kaycee Nicole and *lonelygirl15* were revealed to be hoaxes, readers and viewers were furious. The main reason, of course, was that people felt tricked. They had been treating Kaycee Nicole and Bree as equals, as people like themselves. They had invested emotionally in Kaycee Nicole's illness, and in Bree's difficulties. Many had written heartfelt emails to the characters, had chatted online with Kaycee or recorded video messages for Bree, giving of themselves and offering support and care. This participation goes beyond what we feel for characters we know to be fictional. Yes, we cry over novels and movies, and we sit on the edge of our seats begging horror movie heroines to 'look behind you!' or 'turn on the light!', but we're protected, emotionally, by the knowledge that it's just make-believe. That protection wasn't there for the readers and viewers – and participants – who truly believed that Kaycee Nicole and Bree were real.

A related sense of anger is expressed by Paul Robinett, or, as he is known on YouTube, Renetto. Robinett is a YouTuber who followed *lonelygirl15* eagerly and was horrified to find out that it was a fake. He posted a very emotional video in response to the news. Here's a transcript of some of what he says:

> Look, YouTube is only for people like me, that film in good lighting and in bad lighting, and in my house but in my yard, and you know, I say uh all the time. Uh, and uh. And I don't edit my videos and I don't put really cool music to my videos, like lonelygirl did. No wonder, cos she had a whole freaking production team! No wonder she's like the second most subscribed! And no wonder she gets millions and millions of video views, it's cos she's cheating! And it makes me sick! . . . YouTube's not for fake stuff! It's for real stuff! . . . Kick her off of YouTube, she doesn't belong here. (Robinett 2006)

To Renetto, *lonelygirl15* is cheating, and that's not fair. The point isn't that she's fake, it's that she's gaming the system – 'no wonder she's like the second most subscribed!' Lonelygirl15's fans and Kaycee Nicole's friends thought that they were on an equal footing with these fictional characters. When they found out that they weren't, they felt that they had been used.

Whether they are fictional or not, narratives in blogs differ in several ways from traditional print or cinematic narratives. They are episodic and are published in the same time frame as that of their readers. They are generally not driven towards an ending, towards closure, as traditional narratives are. And, as we have seen in the cases of Kaycee Nicole and lonelygirl15, the boundaries between fiction and hoax are far more shaky – and contentious – than in most traditional narrative. As blogs become more and more common, they may develop more conventions that make them less susceptible to these anxieties about truth and fiction. We may also see more blog narratives that are explicitly fictional (Thomas 2006) and that never attempt to fool their readers.

CHAPTER SIX

Blogging Brands

If you search a bookstore for books on blogging, you'll quickly find that most of them are about how to make money by blogging: *Blog Marketing: The Revolutionary New Method to Increase Sales, Growth, and Profits,* by Jeremy Wright; *Blog: Understanding the Information Reformation that's Changing Your World. Why You Must Know How the Blogosphere Is Smashing the Old Media Monopoly and Giving Individuals Power in the Marketplace of Ideas,* by Hugh Hewitt; *Buzz Marketing with Blogs for Dummies,* by Susannah Gardner; and *Publish & Prosper: Blogging for your Business,* by D. L. Byron and Steve Broback, are just a few of the titles published in recent years. Businesses use blogs in their marketing, as a way of improving customer relations and establishing a popular presence on the Web, or as a way of getting attention. Individual bloggers make money off advertisements on their blogs, often starting blogs about specific topics that they hope will generate lucrative ads and affiliate sales. Spammers create fake blogs, often using software to automatically generate them, creating link farms where the fake blogs link to the Web sites the spammers are trying to hype and that search engines then assume are popular because of all the links.

This chapter explores these uses of blogs, in particular focusing on how blogs work in marketing. We'll look at specific examples of how individuals make their blogs into businesses and how businesses use blogs to connect with customers. First, though, let's consider the way the Web as a participatory medium has changed our expectations as consumers.

The Human Voice

'Markets are conversations.' That phrase is taken from *The Cluetrain Manifesto*, a manifesto of ninety-five theses published online in 1999 by Rick Levine, Chris Locke, Doc Searls and David Weinberger. *Cluetrain*, which was republished as a book the following year, was aimed at businesses operating in the 'newly connected marketplace' of the Internet, but was also broadly read and referenced by bloggers and academics. It argued that the Internet was changing the market and the ways in which consumers communicate about products, and that these changes were occurring a great deal faster than any taking place in the companies trying to sell to that market.

The idea of the Internet as a conversation has been strong ever since, and it is echoed in Robert Scoble and Shel Israel's popular book about corporate blogging, *Naked Conversations* (2006). Thinking about selling something, whether it be news stories, movies, iPods, cars or fashion, by having a conversation is a very different thing from trying to sell something to an audience. As people spend more time online, they spend less time on other media. This means that the tried and tested sales strategies of previous generations – television advertising, for instance – aren't working as well as they used to.

In 1999, advertising online was largely limited to banner ads on popular Web sites. 1999 was also the year when blogging began to become popular, and, by then, Web discussion boards, chat rooms and email had brought the conversational Web to mainstream audiences as well as to the pioneers of Usenet and BBSs. Consumers had begun to turn to each other to discuss products they were considering buying, or had bought, or liked, or hated. Amazon.com had been in business for four years and customers were getting accustomed to comparing other customers' reviews of products before making a purchase. The dot com bubble had not yet burst, and expectations were high.

'Markets are conversations', the first thesis of *The Cluetrain Manifesto* reads, and the list continues: '2. Markets consist of human beings, not demographic sectors. 3. Conversations among human beings sound human. They are conducted in a human voice.' *The Cluetrain Manifesto* is a challenge to corporations to communicate honestly with consumers: '14. Corporations do not speak in the same voice as these new networked conversations. To their intended online audiences, companies sound hollow, flat, literally inhuman. 15. In just a few more years, the current homogenized "voice" of business – the sound of mission statements and brochures – will seem as contrived and artificial as the language of the 18th century French court.'

The Cluetrain Manifesto didn't mention blogs, because blogs, at the time, barely existed. But 'the market' had already become interconnected, with television viewers discussing plot turns with hundreds or thousands of other viewers online, readers writing reviews of books they'd bought at Amazon.com and people discussing good or bad customer service in online discussion groups and mailing lists. *The Cluetrain Manifesto* demanded that big business and big media answer back, in the same human voice that the audiences and consumers were using.

The Cluetrain Manifesto was written from the point of view of consumers who were thrilled with the growing communication with their peers but frustrated at corporations' lack of understanding for these new conversations. *Cluetrain* argues that corporations need to take part in online conversations because these conversations already exist – and if corporations don't get involved, they'll become irrelevant.

Another perspective is voiced by Trevor Cook, a publicist, who argues that blogs finally free corporations to speak directly to consumers, rather than having to always go through the media (Cook 2006). While blogs in many ways liberate corporations from the media, they also mean that publicists need to find different strategies from those they have developed over many years of working with mainstream media. Because publicists have traditionally had to find a way to get the media to publish their stories, they have learnt to focus sharply to attract journalists' attention. Journalists are trained to look for conflicts and inconsistencies, and to find problems. Sensibly enough, journalists don't want to be mouthpieces for corporations, they want journalism to be critical, and so they try to find gaps in the publicists' stories. As Cook points out, the necessary response of publicists is to obsessively eliminate anything negative from the way they represent the products and companies they're trying to sell (Cook 2006, 48). That leads to the hollow, untrustworthy voice of PR that *Cluetrain* argues so strongly against.

Cook argues that, as publicists begin to engage directly with blogs and bloggers instead of reaching the public through the mainstream media, they will have to 'accept some of the roles and responsibilities traditionally associated with good journalism. That means emphasizing qualities like fairness, balance, accuracy, and integrity in our own materials rather than slanted, hyperbolic advocacy that ultimately relies on the third-party endorsement of a trusted media brand for its credibility' (Cook 2006, 52).

Interestingly enough, this connects to our discussion of blogging and journalism in chapter 4. Ultimately, it seems, the question of whether blogging is journalism has to do with money. If you blog to make money, that means your profession is writing and editing: you're a professional writer and editor. In order to maintain the trust of your readers and your own integrity, you will probably find yourself following most of the rules of journalism. And, as we saw in chapter 4, most bloggers do follow basic journalistic rules such as attempting to verify facts and citing their sources (Lenhart and Fox 2006). Looking at the commercial sides of blogging, it is clear that professional bloggers also need to maintain trust, for instance by clearly separating sponsored content from the editorial content, and by maintaining a sense of what Cook calls 'fairness, balance, accuracy, and integrity'.

In the following, we'll explore ways in which individual blog-gers make their blogs into small businesses, earning money from advertising, sponsorship, micropatronage and paid refer-rals. We'll then see how corporations and small businesses have used blogs both in marketing campaigns and in long-term strategies for branding and customer relations. Finally we'll look at some of the cases where commercial blogging has gone wrong and done more harm than good – which brings us back to *The Cluetrain Manifesto*'s authentic human voice, and to Cook's 'fairness, balance, accuracy, and integrity'.

Advertisements on Blogs

There are no corporate blogs among the most popular blogs that are listed on *Technorati*, but most of the most popular blogs are commercial in the sense that they make some amount of money from ads on their blogs. According to a survey conducted by University of Texas researchers in col-laboration with Chitika, a company offering advertising sys-tems for bloggers, bloggers currently make half a billion US dollars (Mookerjee and Dawande 2007). That figure is fairly low considering the global reach of blogs, and the figures are likely to be inaccurate, given that the overall estimates are solely based on earnings for blogs that use the Chitika system. The researchers have simply taken an educated guess at the blogs' other earnings. But when you consider that the first commercial blogs only appeared a few years ago, the earnings estimate from the Chitika survey is noteworthy – and responses from bloggers suggest that they are not far wrong. One interesting point emphasized by the researchers is that blogs don't appear to follow the expected 80/20 rule, where 80 per cent of the money is expected to be earned by 20 per cent of the products or companies. Instead, the top 15 per cent of blogs, based on Technorati's ranking, make 90 per cent of the money. Perhaps that's partly because the long tail of bloggers – the amateurs who simply enjoy blogging – don't bother with ads because they see their blog as a hobby rather than as a profession.

An increasing number of bloggers *are* seeing their blogging as a profession, however. Bloggers who are able to make a living from individually run blogs usually either have a strong personal brand built up over years, or they very carefully seek niche markets to blog about, where advertisements and affiliate programs that match the products they discuss will pay well.

Dooce.com was one of the first blogs that made enough money from advertisements for the blogger to live on a 'comfortable enough middle class to upper-middle class income' (Canham 2006). The first ads Dooce included were text ads, that is, small text-only advertisements, managed by a company called AdBrite that allowed advertisers to buy ads for a particular length of time on a particular Web site. Currently, bloggers are more likely to use contextual ads, where the advertiser and blogger aren't matched per se, but where the ad itself is matched to the content of the Web page displaying the ad. Thus, a blog post about attending a wedding might bring up ads for wedding products and services, whereas a blog post reviewing a digital camera would likely bring up ads related to photography. Ads can additionally be customized to the individual reader's geographic location, which is revealed by your IP number. Google's AdSense, launched in 2003, was the first major program offering bloggers and other Web site owners easy advertising. Google bought Blogger in 2003, and in 2005, AdSense was integrated into Blogger.com's user interface, making it very easy for Blogger users to add advertising to their blogs.

Dooce found, however, that she didn't make enough money from text ads alone, and so in 2005 she added graphical advertisements to her blog as well, which quickly increased her income. She wrote about her reasons for this in a post on September 21 of that year, explaining that she and her husband needed the money and were planning to live on the income from the blog exclusively in a transitional period.

After this rather apologetic section, she gives a more positive rationale as well:

> I also think that right now is a perfect time for me to go for it, to publish myself and make a living while doing it. There are examples out there of 'publishing empires' where one person owns several Internet properties and hires people to maintain those properties for him: car sites, gossip sites, gadget sites, your garden variety boobie sites, etc. You know who they are. What's so exciting about technology and the state of the Internet RIGHT NOW is that I can hire myself and maintain my own property. And so can anyone else, it's just matter of working to make it happen and taking control of the power.

Dooce got a lot of complaints from readers about her decision to add advertisements to the site. Many of the complaints, which she discusses in a post on 1 November 2005, were about the sheer size of the graphical ads, and about their 'ugliness'. Although none of the complaints she cites specifically addresses the idea that the actual writing might change as a result of the blogger accepting advertisements, Dooce does clearly feel the need to address this concern, and she fiercely writes, 'I'd take down my Web site before I'd let an advertiser have any say in my content.' In an earlier post on 19 August 2004, when introducing text ads, Dooce wrote, wittily though poignantly, about 'selling her soul'. It is quite clear that early bloggers going commercial had a lot of conflicts in their minds about changing a labour of love into a living. But despite the reader complaints, if you look at the Alexa.com graph of Dooce.com's readership over time, you'll see that the readership grew significantly in the year or two following the introduction of ads, although 2007 sees somewhat lower figures. The introduction of ads seems to have had a positive effect on readership, if anything.

Today, almost all the top ranking blogs have ads. But it's worth noting that only a handful of personal blogs like Dooce's are listed in the top hundred blogs as Technorati ranks them. The most popular blogs are blogs about gadgets or technology (*Engadget, Gizmodo, TechCrunch, Ars Technica*), about strange and amusing finds (*Boing Boing, PostSecret*) or productivity (*LifeHack*). A little further down the list we see blogs dealing with politics, celebrity gossip, gaming and environmentalism. None of these blogs has a lot in common with the early blogs we looked at in chapter 1, centred as they were on the individual writing them and his or her divergent interests. Today the most popular blogs are deliberately focused on a specific issue or type of post. And almost all the top hundred blogs have ads.

Some commercial blogs make their money by being extremely thorough and serious, such as Darren Rowse's *Digital Photography Blog*. For this site, Rowse and his team simply scour the Web for any new reviews of digital cameras they can find, and post them all, along with a photo of the camera, a brief excerpt from the review, and, of course, a link to a site where you can buy the camera in question, thus earning Rowse a referral fee. Each post follows a completely rigid format, always beginning with '[Magazine or site] has a review of the [camera model], and writes', followed by an extract from the review. The Web site is clearly optimized for search engines and intended to attract readers searching for information while planning to buy a new camera. There are lots of ads, and there is practically no sense of any personality. Rowse runs a number of other blogs as well, including the very popular Problogger.com, which we'll return to later in this chapter.

Other commercial bloggers opt for humour, such as the pseudonymously written *Manolo's Shoe Blog*, where the blogger uses the character Manolo to great effect. While the blogger has never claimed to be Manolo Blahnik, the famous Spanish fashion designer particularly known for his women's shoes, he (or she?) prominently displays a quote from Blahnik on the blog: 'Manolo Blahnik Says "Manolo the Shoeblogger? Sorry, not me. But it's very funny, isn't it? Hilarious!" ' Cleverly enough, this denial from the real Manolo actually adds credibility to the blog – the real Manolo likes the blog! This post from 6 August 2007 is typical of Manolo the shoe-blogger's style. A picture of a pair of shoes is shown with a brief text beneath the image:

> Manolo says, the fall is coming, and it is time to prepare with shoes such as this simple, suede, <u>sling-back peep-toe pump the Kate Spade</u>. Not only is it elegant, but the Manolo thinks it is very smart in these two rich colors, the ruby and the navy.

The link from 'sling-back peep-toe pump the Kate Spade' goes to the item page for these shoes at Zappos.com, an online shoe store that offers so-called associates a 15 per cent cut of the total amount paid by customers they refer. These particular shoes cost US $278, so, each time one of Manolo's readers buys a pair of these shoes after clicking through from his blog, Manolo earns $41.70. If a reader finds that particular pair too expensive, but continues surfing on Zappos.com and buys another pair instead, Manolo receives a 15 per cent cut of whatever the reader paid. In addition to his income from referrals, Manolo has income from ordinary ads on his site. He has contextual ads from Google, with images, and small ads from a number of sites down through his right-hand column. Importantly, Manolo does more than simply provide links to shoes his readers might buy. He also clearly spends a lot of time reading other blogs about fashion, and generously links to other bloggers, and often to bloggers who are not particularly well known or commercialized. This active social networking is important in building a community of active readers, who not only read Manolo's blog, but also leave comments, blog about Manolo on their own blogs and, of course, buy shoes.

Micropatronage

Around the same time as Dooce introduced advertisements, Jason Kottke chose another strategy for making a living off blogging. On 22 February 2005, he made an announcement on his blog kottke.org: 'I recently quit my Web design gig and – as of today – will be working on kottke.org as my full-time job. And I need your help.' Kottke explained that he was asking regular readers to become 'micropatrons' of the site by contributing a small donation. He did not set up formal subscriptions or limit access to the site for non-contributing readers, but simply left it up to readers to decide what they'd like to do. The reason for doing this was that he'd found blogging to be increasingly time-consuming and that it put a drain on other important parts of his life, so he had considered quitting. But blogging also gave him a great deal of pleasure: 'this little hobby of mine has been the most rewarding, pleasurable, maddening, challenging thing in my life'. The problem, he'd decided, was not that he wanted to quit blogging, but that he didn't want to have to deal with two jobs: blogging and the Web design job he was paid to do. He also saw it as an experiment to find ways of professionalizing blogging without accepting advertisements, and as an experiment in a new kind of patronage suited to our time: hence micropatronage where each reader pays a small amount rather than having a single, very wealthy sponsor or patron, as was common for artists in the Renaissance. This is a similar approach to that taken by Christopher Allbritton, the independent journalist who used reader donations to fund a trip to Iraq in 2003 (see chapter 4).

Kottke did manage to make enough money in donations to support himself for a year – at a little less than a third of the income that he had received from his Web design job (Kottke.org, 10 April 2005). As he admitted on his blog when the year was up, 'about 1450 micropatrons contributed $39,900' (22 February 2006). However, less than one in three hundred of his monthly readers contributed as micropatrons, and he anticipated that any future fund drives would be less successful, as many contributors had in a sense been offering back payment for the seven years Kottke had already been blogging. That led him actually to recommend advertising to others as a more sustainable model, which in some ways matches Dooce's argument, posted to her blog on 1 November 2005, for using advertising rather than a subscription model or something akin to micropatronage: 'By using ads I'm making my livelihood my problem and no one else's.'

When Kottke decided not to attempt to live off his blog for a second year, he gave the following reason: 'The day that kottke.org becomes a real business that focuses on profit first (instead of the pseudo-business labor-of-love it is now) is the day the site will probably start to suck' (10 April 2005). Despite the limited successes of Allbritton and Kottke in funding their blogging projects through many small reader donations, few bloggers after them have attempted to copy their example. Instead, bloggers wanting to monetize their blogs, as the jargon has it, generally turn to advertising, sponsored posts and affiliate links.

Sponsored Posts and Pay-to-Post

Micropatronage and ads surround the blog but can, in theory, leave the posts and the blogger's integrity intact. When actual blog posts are sponsored, questions of trust and integrity arise. The first high-profile example of sponsored posts arose in December 2004, when a group of fifteen high-profile bloggers was recruited by Marqui, a company that made a content management system, to write weekly posts linking to the company's site. The company did not require the post to be positive about their product. In return, they would pay the bloggers US $800 per month. Most of the bloggers quit after their three-month contracts were up, some with no comment, but several writing that it had made the whole process of blogging difficult for them. In late 2004 and early 2005, the sponsored Marqui posts caused a lot of debate. On 5 December 2004, Steve Boyd wrote on his blog *Get Real* that the paid bloggers were 'squandering the trust that people have for them'. Molly E. Holzschlag, one of the Marqui bloggers, decided not to renew her contract with Marqui because it changed the way she felt about blogging: 'Primarily, I learned that I can't blog naturally if I feel forced to do it, and that's intriguing because I can write in just about any style. But, it turns out my blog is really personal, I take it personally, and I need it to be that way' (Molly.com, 28 February 2005). Holzschlag's site is – according to the first page you see when you type http://molly.com into your browser – a site that shares her 'Web development work and personal thoughts'. It is not primarily a diary-style site, and yet she found that her blog was 'really personal'.

The divide between editorial content and sponsored ads is strict in conventional journalism. When bloggers blur that line by accepting payment to write about a product or company, they break with the cultural expectations set by journalism. There have been many examples of mainstream media getting into trouble for blurring the line. One of the most famous is the payola scandal in the USA in the 1950s, when it became apparent that radio stations were being paid by the record companies to play particular music, thus making that music more popular. Today payola is illegal in the United States, unless there is full disclosure by the radio station that the music in question is sponsored.

Blogging is an unregulated area, and this is the sort of question that shows that blogging is not simply a form of journalism. It is not clear whether blogging should follow the rules of mainstream media about separating editorial content from sponsored content, and even if there were an agreement about this, there would be no way to make bloggers follow it. J. D. Lasica argues straight out that a blogger who wishes to be thought of as a journalist cannot post sponsored entries: 'If bloggers are paid by a corporation to write about the company, they're no longer acting as amateur journalists. Journalists cannot and do not accept payments from sources' (Lasica 2005). But, as we saw in chapter 4, only about 34 per cent of bloggers think of themselves as journalists (Lenhart and Fox 2006).

The Marqui blog-sponsoring was a limited experiment for bloggers who had been individually recruited. By 2006, however, there were several systems that aimed to act as brokers between bloggers willing to write for money and advertisers

wishing to find bloggers to promote their products. PayPerPost
has been one of the most controversial but also one of the most
successful.

As a blogger, you sign up for PayPerPost, and then have
access to a list of tens or hundreds of 'opportunities' that are
available. Sometimes these are very specific about what they
want blog posts to look like, like this listing from October 2006:

> The post should describe about culture and how marriage
> affects culture. It should cover the topics., 1) Is Marriage
> Really needed? 2) Asians gives more value to marriage, For
> example in India, I see that Online matrimonial Portals are
> making a great income. For example, i came across,
> Bharatmatrimony.com, It seems to be the leader of online
> Matrimonial services. 3) They try several innovative ideas,
> like, launching of the First matrimonial toolbar, Also
> Provides RSS feeds., Even yahoo has shown an interest on
> them and has invested in them.

A Technorati search at the time suggested that this attempt at
generating buzz wasn't all that successful: not many blogs
linked to the site. However, a year later, over 200 blogs did so.
Most of these had low authority on Technorati – that is, not
many other blogs linked to them – and many of the blogs
seemed like spam, offering little but lists of links, it being
unclear whether these new links were caused by PayPerPost or
other strategies. Other 'opportunities' offered at PayPerPost
that month asked you to plug a javascript into your blog post so
they can pay extra money for each click-through. There's an x-
mas gift service, for instance, specifying that in your post you
need to include both a javascript that will automatically show
the service's top-selling gifts as well as a sentence about how
'bloggers will be making money this Christmas, and not just
on PayPerPost!'

In their first months, PayPerPost received a lot of criticism
for their service, in particular because they didn't, at that point,
require bloggers to disclose that they were being sponsored.
In fact, some of the 'opportunities' bloggers were offered

specifically required that the blogger not mention that he or she accepted payment for posts. After heavy criticism, PayPerPost revised their policies, and now require that bloggers disclose that they accept money for posts, although bloggers may choose whether to do that on a post-by-post basis or with a single badge for the whole site, stating that they accept sponsored posts. The rationale given for this policy is precisely the need to maintain readers' trust, as stated in the 'Code of Ethics' posted to the PayPerPost Web site:

> Your readers trust you. PayPerPost is committed to keeping it that way. That's why we insist on a strict policy of full-disclosure when you discuss an advertiser's product or service on your blog. By receiving payment for blogging about a certain topic, even if you would have written about that topic anyway, you run the risk of giving the impression of a conflict of interest. By showing your audience, in a very visible and proactive manner, that you are being paid for that content, you will maintain the trust of your readers and avoid any appearance of impropriety.

Many bloggers have been critical of PayPerPost, and yet the service continues to be successful. Blogger Lynn Terry offers one of the more nuanced positive perspectives on PayPerPost in a post to her blog *ClickNewz!* on 6 October 2006:

> Individual blogs . . . rise and fall on their own accord. If the writer consistently produces bad content, the blog will fail due to lack of readership. If the writer consistently produces great content, the blog will be a success because of that. Whether or not they choose to disclose revenue sources has no real impact on whether the content is good, or whether its bad. The bloggers that will rise to the top and gain substantial readership are those that have great writing style and always give an honest opinion – even if it is just an opinion, and whether its objective or not.

This ignores the non-human readers of blogs. Search engines trawl blogs and other Web sites for metadata that can help sort Web sites according to how good they are, so that the best sites can be shown at the top of the list of results you get when you search online. One important measure search engines use is the number of other sites that link to a site. If a hundred blogs link to your site, it's probably more interesting or important than a site that only has three blogs linking to it. Spammers create fake blogs or fake comments that link to the sites they're trying to push. Search engines and spam filters are, however, getting better at finding machine-generated blogs and comments, and, if caught, spammers are likely to have all their sites banned from the search engine, which renders them practically invisible online. So marketers prefer human-written content to surround the links to their sites – that way, search engines will count the links as genuine endorsements rather than as spam. Whether or not a blog has readers, and whether or not those possible readers lose faith in the blogger, search engines will continue to read the links as endorsements, and so the poorly written, dishonest blog posts bought for $3 on PayPerPost will still be valuable to marketers who simply want to game the search engines.

Corporate Blogs

Businesses that establish blogs come from the other side of the system. Businesses that blog generally don't want to 'monetize' a blog through ads or sponsorship – instead, they want to use the blog to boost an existing income stream by generating new attention for their products or services. Businesses blog to attract attention to their products and to establish themselves as experts, thus building trust and credibility. Ultimately, they blog to attract customers.

Blogging began as a personal, individual form of publication, and successful corporate blogs tend to preserve that sense of personality. Many of the most popular corporate blogs belong to very small businesses, where readers can get a sense of the individuals who run the business. Larger companies often run a group of blogs for different topics, and either assign writers to each blog or set up group blogs where employees take turns at writing. Very large companies, such as Microsoft or Google, have no single, official corporate blog, but encourage their employees to start their own blogs, where they write about their professional interests.

I mentioned *Manolo's Shoe Blog* earlier in this chapter. Another famous fashion blogger is Thomas Mahon, a London tailor who specializes in hand-made men's suits. In their popular book on corporate blogging, *Naked Conversations*, Robert Scoble and Shel Israel describe how Mahon expanded his business through blogging, carefully coached by the ex-advertising executive Hugh MacLeod. Mahon's blog, *English Cut*, has no advertisements – this blog is about connecting with potential customers and establishing Mahon as an expert in his field. The first posts in the blog explain the business. Mahon explains what a bespoke suit is, and the difference between such a suit and made-to-measure suits or off-the-rack suits. He shows photos of his workshop, of patterns being drafted and fabric being cut. He explains specialities of the different tailors on Savile Row, and tells us his prices. Later posts are then able to build upon this and frequently link back to these basics when appropriate. As Scoble and Shel note, 'Mahon, wisely, didn't try to sell suits on the new blog. Instead, he showed his knowledge and love of the craft. He explained the labor and why the cost was justified' (2006, 65). Recent posts on *English Cut* have included discussions of the qualities of various wools, an introduction to a new addition to the tailor's staff and a long, musing post about the care and time involved in crafts such as tailoring.

There are many reasons to blog. In general, blogging is a way of communicating directly with customers without having to use the media as an intermediary. More specifically, blogs allow companies to establish themselves as experts in a field, to engage directly in ongoing conversations among their customers or to start their own conversations. Blogs are a way corporations try to create a 'human voice', as the authors of *The Cluetrain Manifesto* would have said.

Mahon succeeded in establishing himself as an expert in his field through his blog. If you type 'tailor London' into a search engine, Mahon will show up at the top of the list. If fact, even leaving London out of your search terms, you'll see Mahon's blog in the first few hits. Mahon explains his craft using simple language and photographs. He even, in posts like 'If You Can't Afford Bespoke' (19 January 2005), gives advice on more reasonably priced suit-purchases for people who can't afford his £2000 suits. Posts like these give readers insight into a craft that for many has seemed completely inaccessible, and in this way he builds a much broader reputation for himself than would be possible with traditional means of advertising. He also keeps his existing customers engaged in the process while they're waiting for their suits to be completed (it takes about three months), for instance by explaining how they mark suits at a fitting, and how they make alterations based on these marks. Selling custom-made suits is a niche business – Mahon is never going to have millions of customers. Through blogging though, Mahon has succeeded in expanding what used to be a largely local business, giving it global reach. As Scoble and Israel write, 'It's still a word-of-mouth business, but blogging has scaled it to global levels' (*The English Cut* 2006, 66).

Another reason businesses might want to blog is in order to participate in the conversations about them already taking place online. Mike Torres, the lead program manager for MSN Spaces, talks about this in an interview in *Naked Conversations*. Torres says he runs regular searches on Technorati for keywords related to MSN Spaces, and, when he finds bloggers discussing it, he jumps into the conversation. 'It stops the rants. A lot of times when you do that, there's a "Sorry – I didn't know you were listening" reply. One guy posted, "Big retraction: I was wrong." What happens is that if they know you're in the conversation, people get respectful. They may still criticise you, but they don't lie' (Scoble and Israel 2006, 20).

Many businesses have used similar strategies. You may have heard of the SEO or search engine optimization industry.

Basically, search engine optimizers tweak Web sites to make them as findable as possible. Sometimes methods are not entirely ethical, as when spammers create link farms – that is, multiple Web sites with no real content except for links pointing to the sites that are being 'optimized'. Another hated method is to leave comment spam on blogs, with links to the same sites but no real content in the comments. Google and other search engines have strict rules against these strategies, and punish those who are seen as spammers and link farmers by completely excluding their Web sites from the search index.

Sometimes this strategy can target innocent Web sites, as in the case of TalkOrigins.org, a Web site that had the misfortune to be hacked by someone who added a hidden list of links to suspect link-farming sites into the source code. The webmaster didn't notice that this had happened, as the Web site still looked the same as before – but then he discovered that Google was no longer indexing his site. He could not find any information about *why* his site had been made invisible to anyone searching Google, but eventually found the hacked code and removed it. At 3 am on 3 December 2006, the webmaster wrote an angry blog post describing his dilemma on his blog Austringer.net. In particular, he complained that Google had not provided any information about what the problem was and that there was no way to contact Google to get this information.

At 11:21 pm the same day, Slashdot.org, the popular news site for technology people that we discussed in chapter 4, had picked up the story and posted it with the title 'Google De-indexes Talk.Origins, Won't Say Why'. *Slashdot* is such a popular site that being 'Slashdotted', or featured on *Slashdot*, will often crash a small Web site's server, which won't be set up for the hordes of visitors coming from *Slashdot*. And Google noticed: less than three-and-a-half hours after the *Slashdot* post, Matt Cutts, head of the Webspam team at Google, blogged in response: 'If you've never read my blog before, welcome. I'm the head of the Webspam team at Google. And I have a blog for days just like this.' (Mattcutts.com, 4 December

2006). Cutts provides links both to the original post from Talk.Origins' webmaster and to the *Slashdot* story. He goes on to explain exactly how Google had handled the issues at Talk.Origin, and explains how they tried to email the webmaster. He also apologizes, saying that Google is working at doing a better job of this, but also affirms that he believes Google already does a far better job than any other search engine.

Individual disgruntled customers can have a lot of power today through posting their complaints on their blog – or, even more damningly, by posting videos or audio recordings of bad customer service. A popular example is the video a customer posted to YouTube of a visiting Comcast technician asleep on the customer's couch, waiting on hold to speak to Comcast's repair office for assistance with the repair he was working on (Doorframe 2006). That video spread like wildfire, and also got attention from mainstream media (Belson 2006). Other consumers start fan blogs for brands they love, such as *Barq's*, a blog about *Barq's Root Beer* that is analysed both in Ben McConnell and Jackie Huba's *Citizen Marketers* (2007) and by Robert Kozinets (2006).

Mahon's blog is an example of the leader of a small business writing a blog profiling his company and himself. Cutt's blog is an example of a prominent person in a very large company writing a blog about his work. More and more, large companies like Google are encouraging their employees to blog. Robert Scoble, who was a Microsoft employee when he and Shel Israel wrote *Naked Conversations* (2006), writes enthusiastically about the large number of Microsoft employees who blog, even arguing that their blogging has shifted the general opinion of Microsoft as the 'evil empire' to a much more positive customer opinion (Scoble and Israel 2006, 10–11).

Big companies use blogs in different ways. Individual employees may run their own, personally branded sites that also discuss their job. Matt Cutts' blog does not have a google.com URL, instead he blogs at mattcutts.com. However, he clearly states that he works at Google, and most of his posts are in some way related to his job. Other companies set up group blogs where several employees take turns at blogging. Or blogs can be set up about different topics, as at Arla, the largest Danish dairy, which has separate blogs for recipes, for environmental issues concerning milk production, for consumer issues, and, most creatively, for two farmers who supply milk to the dairy.

Some companies post guidelines for bloggers. Sometimes these guidelines represent a total ban on blogging, as for members of the Australian military from December 2006 and of the British military from August 2007 (bbc.co.uk 2007). In May 2007, the US army first issued what appeared to be a similar ban, and then, days later, loosened these restrictions, stating that 'In no way will every blog post/update a Soldier makes on his or her blog need to be monitored or first approved by an immediate supervisor' (Griffin 2007). However, blogs must be registered and will be spot-checked at certain intervals. While soldiers' blogs have revealed poor conditions, others have been excellent advertising for the army – quite apart from the unique historical record created by these correspondences.

At the opposite extreme, we have Microsoft's policy on blogging as reported in *Naked Conversations* – at the time the book was written, they had no policy. That doesn't mean the legal department hadn't worried about it (Scoble and Israel 2006, 12), but, as Steve Ballmer says in *Naked Conversations*, 'We trust our people to represent our company. That's what they're paid to do. If they didn't want to be here, they wouldn't be here. So in a sense you don't run any more risk letting someone express themselves on a blog than you do letting them go out and see a customer on their own' (19). Of course, Microsoft's employees have chosen their jobs, and they can quit at any time. The latter is a luxury not afforded to most soldiers. Since then, guidelines for 'Successful Blogging' have been released at Microsoft, with a fairly simple list of rules, as reported by Debbie Weil at her blog *BlogWrite for CEOs* (25 January 2005). For instance, employees are asked to 'Respect existing confidentiality agreements', to 'Identify yourself', 'Speak for yourself' and 'Think about reactions before you post'.

The Walker Art Center is an example of a company that provides liberal but clear guidelines for their bloggers, and in the interest of full disclosure and trust they have chosen to make their guidelines available to their readers as well (Walker Art Center, 2006). In part, the guidelines simply remind bloggers not to break the law: 'Do not post material that is unlawful, abusive, defamatory, invasive of another's privacy, or obscene to a reasonable person.' There are also points that may be obvious to someone used to blogging, but could be useful for newcomers: 'Get permission from colleagues before writing about them.' Some of the guidelines simply give basic advice on blogging style and etiquette, asking bloggers to provide links when quoting sources, for instance.

Engaging Bloggers

Micropatronage, sponsored posts and advertising on blogs are all ways in which individuals are able to set themselves up as independent writers who can make money from their writing. Most make very little, but some bloggers have succeeded in making a living from their blogs (Glasner 2006, Rowse 2007).

But, from the point of view of the advertisers, these strategies are neither revolutionary nor necessarily particularly profitable. As Renee Blodgett told J. D. Lasica, 'most of the marketing world has decided to take a different approach: Instead of paying bloggers, you establish relationships and engage those bloggers who care deeply about the industry that impacts you or your clients' (Lasica 2005). This is the approach taken by Stormhoek, a small South African winery that has become a prime example of a company that has successfully leveraged blogging – in the two years since they started blogging, their sales increased five-fold, an increase they attribute primarily to blogging, according to a post to Hugh MacLeod's blog *GapingVoid* on 29 December 2006. Interestingly enough,

MacLeod is Stormhoek's blogging consultant – the same MacLeod was also the man who helped Thomas Mahon the tailor start his successful blog. In a video posted to the company blog, Stormhoek director Jason Korman says the following:

> With the incredible power of social software, why would you ever buy an ad? If you have something interesting to say online today, so many people will pick it up. A lot of what online marketing is about is having a mess of stuff out there so when people are interested in the brand, there are 1,000 things they can click on. (Davis 2006)

When Manolo links to other fashion blogs, he engages in conversations that are already occurring. The links are useful and entertaining to his readers, who thus find more blogs that interest them. Simultaneously, Manolo gains the good will of the bloggers he links to, who are then more likely to return the favour and link back to him – ultimately getting him more readers, which again leads to more money. When Thomas Mahon explains the origin of the phrase 'no strings attached' by showing us a piece of beautiful silk, just received from the cloth merchant, with little strings tied to its almost imperceptible flaws (*The English Cut*, 1 April 2005), he shares a small piece of knowledge packaged in a way that is easy for other bloggers to link to and share with their readers – thus gaining himself more readers.

Stormhoek takes things a step further by giving readers tasks to solve. In August 2007, the winery promised a £5 voucher to the first 500 readers to send in photos of themselves buying a bottle of Stormhoek wine. Running contests and promising consumers freebies is, of course, hardly a new marketing strategy, but the way this is presented on the Stormhoek blog makes it sound very down-to-earth: 'This might turn out to be quite groovy, it might not. Whatever. Fail fast, fail often etc. But it's a cool enough idea to make it worth a try' (7 June 2007). Stormhoek specifically doesn't want to look polished. As the director of Stormhoek said in the video, 'that sanitized, carefully produced life view wineries have tried to portray, people just aren't buying it anymore. Life just isn't like that' (Davis 2006).

Another twist on this idea has been used by Darren Rowse at ProBlogger.com, who engaged readers by organizing a project called '31 Days to Building a Better Blog', where he posted daily tips on improving your blog, and additionally asked readers to post their own tips on their own blogs. If readers submitted their posts to ProBlogger.com by filling out a Web-based form, Rowse promised to link back to their posts. There was no requirement that participants must link to ProBlogger.com.

Rowse achieved several things through this. It was a generous move, in that his coordination of the project gathered valuable information for bloggers trying to improve their blogs with the aim to make more money from them. He linked to participants, and, as ProBlogger.com is highly ranked on Technorati and other search engines, links from the site are valuable. Bloggers receiving links will not only have new readers who have followed the link, they'll also gain a higher rating on search engines because they've been linked from an influential Web site. Of course, the project is clearly also to Rowse's own advantage. By activating readers, he will gather a valuable resource that is likely to attract many readers. Although he doesn't require links from participants, most probably will link to him, which gets him new readers and higher scores on search engines. By taking the lead in such a project, his status as an expert is augmented. And he has a clear agenda for what he will blog about for a whole month.

Sites like ProBlogger.com regularly post lists of tactics for getting more readers, and readers who will return again and again. Interestingly enough, such lists are in themselves very popular blog posts that gain a lot of attention from other bloggers – the business of making money by blogging is one of the most lucrative topics to blog on, it appears. Be that as it may, the advice given is clearly presented and well received, and applicable to those who wish to make money from their blogs, those who wish to establish themselves as experts, or those who simply enjoy the social aspects of blogging. The main advice is simply to engage with your readers. If readers leave comments, then respond yourself. Visit other blogs that are about the same topic as yours, and leave comments there – and link to interesting posts on their blogs. Some recommend more intense strategies, such as emailing new commentators and thanking them for reading your blog. Others have daily targets: visit five new blogs a day and leave comments on them. Link to three new blogs each week.

The basic point is simple, though: blogs are a social form of writing, and don't work well in a vacuum. Some blogs can survive on transitory readers, who simply arrive from a search – Darren Rowse's *Digital Photography Blog* is an example. This kind of blog doesn't need to have a personal style or to establish relationships with other blogs, because it is unlikely that many readers will return once their camera is bought. If they do return, it is entirely for the information given on the site. Many blogs want to build a brand though, and, in order to achieve that, you want readers to return again and again, and you want other Web sites to link to your blog in order to attract new readers. This requires engaging with your readers and with other bloggers, who often are your readers as well.

Corporate Blogging Gone Wrong

People expect blogs to be honest and authentic. You can see that in Dooce's insistence that she will never allow her sponsors and advertisers to affect the content of her blog, and you can see it in bloggers' concerns about PayPerPost and the necessity of disclosure. When readers discover that bloggers they have been reading break with this expectation, the backlash can be enormous.

A Wal-Mart sponsored blog that didn't disclose its sponsorship is a good example of a blog that didn't tell the entire truth. *Wal-Marting Across America* was a blog written by a couple who were driving an RV across the United States and staying overnight in Wal-Mart parking lots. The blog has since been deleted, with just a single post left to explain the story. The author, who calls herself simply Laura, writes that she and her husband had originally planned to do the trip as a vacation, and, since she's a freelance writer, she wanted to write an article about it for an RV magazine. She asked Wal-Mart for permission in advance, and was thrilled when they offered to sponsor the couple if they blogged their trip. Unfortunately, they didn't disclose the sponsorship – and their blog was full of interviews with Wal-Mart employees who were unanimously happy with their jobs. Unsurprisingly, other bloggers failed to believe that the blog was authentic – it seemed too good to be true. Working conditions at Wal-Mart are such a contentious issue that anything that's that positive about the company is closely watched by organizations like *Wal-Mart Watch*.

The original blog posts have since been taken offline altogether and removed from archive.org, but *Business Week* quotes a sample blog post, titled 'From Cashier to Manager':

> Now Felicia is a Project Manager for Corporate Strategy/ Sustainability and is very proud of Wal-Mart's efforts to protect the environment. . . . Wal-Mart is working toward an energy use goal of 100% renewable resources; targeting zero waste from packaging by 2025 and selling products that are good for the world. (Gogoi 2006)

Richard Edelman, the CEO of the advertising company behind Working Families for Wal-Mart, the organization that sponsored the blog, was heavily criticized for the flop because he has spoken out often about the need for transparency and honesty in this kind of marketing. In fact, Edelman is a leading member of the Word of Mouth Marketing Association (WOMMA), which has developed strict ethical guidelines that its members commit to following. There are even specific ethical principles for marketers to follow when contacting bloggers. At the top of the list of principles, it says: 'Consumers come first, honesty isn't optional, and deception is always exposed.' The *Wal-Marting Across America* debacle tends to confirm that.

The specific issue at stake in the case was the lack of disclosure: it was not made clear that Laura and her husband Jim's trip was fully sponsored and that they were being paid a salary in order to write the blog (Gogoi 2006). Jim and Laura were presented as just ordinary people with no special interests. This is specifically addressed in the WOMMA ethical guidelines in the section on 'Honesty of Identity', which states that 'Campaign organizers should monitor and enforce disclosure of identity. Manner of disclosure can be flexible, based on the context of the communication. Explicit disclosure is not required for an obviously fictional character, but would be required for an artificial identity or corporate representative that could be mistaken for an average consumer.' An obviously fictional character might be a character in a television drama or Barbie – yes, the doll – who also had her own blog for a while. Jim and Laura could, however, definitely be mistaken for average consumers rather than fictional or even sponsored characters.

In later interviews, Richard Edelman apologized for the dishonesty in the *Wal-Marting Across America* project. He also explained that the case had shown the importance of ethical training for all members of staff, as the people who had handled this particular case obviously hadn't followed the ethical guidelines the company was committed to.

If nothing else, the *Wal-Marting Across America* blog and the resulting backlash show the importance of realizing that ethical guidelines such as those put forward by WOMMA are necessary, and an accurate estimate of most bloggers' and consumers' sense of justice.

Another way marketers have fallen into the trap of dishonesty is through apparent payola. Some companies have sent bloggers free gadgets – digital cameras, computers and the like – for review, much as they might do to the mainstream media. This has led to accusations against the bloggers who received these goodies and wrote about them. On *Slashdot*, the review copies of computers from Microsoft were seen as 'bribes' (27 December 2006), and in fact some bloggers, like Brandon

LeBlanc of *MSTechToday*, did write enthusiastically about the computer without disclosing that it had been a free gift from Microsoft. When found out, LeBlanc was viciously attacked by his readers, in comments to his posts of 23 December and 27 December 2006. Only a small number of commentators appeared to believe that he should have sent the computer back. What really irked readers was that LeBlanc hadn't told the whole truth from the beginning.

Nikon tried to avoid this problem in 2007 by sending 50 bloggers their latest and best model of digital camera, but on loan rather than as a free gift (or bribe, as some would argue). Bloggers who received the cameras had three options: send it back after six months, apply for a second six-month loan, or buy it at a discount, the money going to charity. One of the selected bloggers, Mack Collier, who writes the blog *The Viral Garden*, wrote that the reason he accepted Nikon's offer was their emphasis on honesty and transparency. He quoted the letter from Nikon in a post to his blog on 18 April 2007: 'There is only one requisite for receiving this camera: Should you decide to talk about your experience with the D80 we send you, in any forum, you must let people know that you got the camera on loan from Nikon. We want you to be as candid and transparent as possible about where you got this camera and what you're doing with it.' By emphasizing their desire for full disclosure and honesty, Nikon reassures bloggers that they are not trying to buy their souls or disrupt their integrity – and they additionally got good press from bloggers applauding their insistence on full disclosure.

Truth and integrity are at the core of both the success stories and the failures of commercial blogging. Conventions for displaying truth and integrity have long been established in journalism, marketing and face to face communication. They are still in the process of being established in blogging. Although many mistakes have been made, conventions do exist, as evidenced by the WOMMA guidelines and by the similarly outraged response of blog readers when the basic trust is broken and a blog that has been presented as authentic turns out to be a marketing construction or fictional or heavily sponsored.

As *The Cluetrain Manifesto* asserted, honest conversation and the human voice are at the heart of successful blogging. While this idea may have been neglected in the Gutenberg parenthesis of print and mass media, it is not by any means a new idea. As we discussed in chapter 2, Plato held that a dialogue with worthy listeners and the careful tending of communication is the best way to spread your ideas. If Plato were a marketing professional rather than a philosopher, we might imagine his being quite pleased with the way corporations are realigning their communication to a dialogue-based model.

CHAPTER SEVEN

The Future of Blogging

So will we still be blogging in twenty years' time? What about in fifty years' time, or a hundred? Blogging is only a decade old, and it's too early yet to know how well it will weather the decades to come, but there are trends that seem likely to continue.

People like participating in the media. We like contributing and sharing our ideas, and we're unlikely to stop now that we have the technology to allow it. Participatory media that makes publishing available to everyone is like fire: once the cunning Prometheus had stolen the secret of fire from Zeus and given it to us mortals, there was no way for the gods to take it back. Countries such as Iran and China have tried to block blogging and social networks but without much luck. Iranians in particular insist on blogging despite their government's attempts at suppressing it; in fact, Farsi is now among the top ten languages used on blogs (Sifry 2007). With technology getting cheaper and easier to use, we're likely to continue to see shared media of all kinds – text, audio, still images and videos – and in more parts of the world between more groups of people. Participation in participatory media is still obviously limited by access to technology, to the Internet and to the time and skills to use these. But more and more nations are participating. The ethnic and gender distribution of bloggers is also encouraging. In the United States, Pew Internet found that the ethnic distribution of bloggers was more balanced than that of the general Internet population (Lenhart and Fox 2006). The distribution of men and women is also fairly even (Herring et al. 2004, Lenhart and Fox

2006), particularly among younger age groups. This is promising for the future.

Blogging may not remain a separate activity or genre, as it is
today. In the last few years, we've seen blogging spread into
social network sites, and in some cases merge with them, as
discussed in chapter 3. Karl Long of the blog *ExperienceCurve*
described Facebook as nothing more than 'a blog template' in
a post on 12 August 2007, and certainly Facebook incorporates
many aspects of blogging: posts are ordered in reverse chronological order, there is an emphasis on the individual and the
subjective. Facebook also automates many of the social networking functions that have been built around blogs. Where
blogs use RSS feeds, Trackbacks and external blog indices
like Technorati, Facebook simply includes all this in a single
system. People blog on YouTube, with each entry being a new
short video. Perhaps we won't use the word blogging in twenty
years' time, but it seems likely that a form of personal publication, with links, social networking and brief posts will remain.

Implicit Participation

When we talk about blogging, we usually think about the
posts and comments that people write deliberately. But user-
generated content is more than blog posts, images and videos.
The most valuable information may be that which is implied
rather than deliberately posted. Let me give you an example.
Last.fm is a Web site that, with the help of a small piece of software you install on your computer, tracks the music you listen
to and recommends new bands and songs based on what you
listen to on your own computer. You can also listen to songs on
Last.fm's streaming music radio, where you can mark songs
according to whether you love them or hate them. Additionally,
Last.fm is a social network, so you can connect with friends
and see what music they're listening to – and, of course, you
can have Last.fm automatically publish a constantly updated
list of songs you've recently listened to on your blog. Users of

Last.fm don't contribute content, they contribute information about which songs they like to listen to. The value here is in the links. If 90 out of 100 users who like the song X also like the song Y, Last.fm can safely recommend Y to a new user who just listened to X but has never heard Y.

This implicitly contributed information is data that can be mined for information that is more valuable than the individual contributions. Google uses the links between blogs and other Web sites as signs of peer recognition, mining our linking data in order to provide us with good search results. Other companies also mine data you barely consider that you've contributed: Amazon to give recommendations, Flickr to show the 'interestingness' of photos, and Technorati to show the most popular blogs or videos. In a post to *O'Reilly Radar* on 15 June 2007, Tim O'Reilly argues that using this data is 'harnessing collective intelligence'. Collective intelligence doesn't lie in the individual videos on YouTube, or in each separate blog post we write, it's in the patterns we trace as we move through these media: the order in which we listen to songs, the books we buy after viewing a particular site, the links we make or the links we choose to follow.

We've only just begun to mine these patterns for their data. In years to come, presumably the recommendations and understandings of what is valuable will be far more nuanced and sophisticated than they are today.

Perils of Personalized Media

Perhaps blogs, Facebook, YouTube and their ilk will simply take over and become the dominant media. Will conventional news organizations like the *New York Times* or the BBC or Reuters even exist ten years from now? Not according to the video *EPIC 2014*, an eight-minute Flash video created by Robin Sloan and Matt Thompson (2004) and presented as though told from the year 2014. The video begins by telling the story of participatory media up until 2004 – the invention of the Web, Amazon.com and its recommendation system, blogging, Google News and so on. But in 2005, the year after the video was actually made, history begins to change. Google buys Amazon, becoming Googlezon and thereby merging Amazon's social filtering with Google's immense databases. Googlezon creates the Google Grid, which allows users to put all their life online. Microsoft launches its own competing systems. And by 2014, the way we find and share information has changed. Here is a transcript of part of the video's voiceover:

> On Sunday, March 9, 2014, Googlezon unleashes EPIC. Welcome to our world. The Evolving Personalized Information Construct is the system by which our sprawling, chaotic mediascape is filtered, ordered and delivered. Everyone contributes now, from blog entries to phone cam images to video reports to full investigations. Many people get paid too, a tiny cut of Google's immense advertising revenue proportional to the popularity of their contributions. EPIC produces a custom content package for each user, uses his choices – his consumption habits, his interests, his demographics, his social network – to shape the product.

This might not sound so bad. And it's not so far off, either. Although Google doesn't own the world to the extent that EPIC 2014 suggests, they did, as noted in the video, buy Blogger.com. In 2006 they bought YouTube. Today I have a Google account that not only gives me email, it also knows which blogs I read and tells me when they're updated. It hosts my personal calendar, my to-do list and several of the documents and spreadsheets I'm working on. I've installed a Google toolbar that allows Google to track every single Web site I visit, giving me handy reports in return and helping me find those sites that I somehow lose though I'm sure I've seen them somewhere. Using this information, Google gives me personalized news. So far, the personalization doesn't seem very advanced. It knows to recommend news items about blogs, but apart from that it doesn't seem to know me as well as I would have expected, given all the data I constantly feed it. And clearly I'm giving up a lot of privacy for these services, as are other users who have signed up.

Even if you haven't signed up for all of Google's services, Google knows a good deal about you. Google saves information about every single search, and connects information about search terms used and which links were followed to the IP number the search was performed from. IP numbers can tell you a lot about an individual. Some universities, for instance, have IP numbers that translate to exact locations, such as (these are made up examples) dorm-room-231.univ-of-catalumbia. edu, student-pc-lab-23.humanities.ubilt.edu.au or even, sometimes, something like jillwalkerrettberg-room271.humanities. uib.no. Even when IP numbers are less revealing than this, they do announce your location, usually specifying the town you're in and your Internet Service Provider. If you're curious to see what your IP address is, go to a site like whatismyipaddress.com or search for 'what is my ip' and you'll find sites that will tell you, even placing you on a map.

But the customization that you get in return for the lost privacy can be extremely useful. I love it when Google finds news items for me that I'm actually interested in, or when Amazon recommends a book I wasn't aware of but realize I really want to read.

Used well, services such as the imagined EPIC 2014 might be far more powerful than traditional newspapers and television. But they also give cause for concern. Here is another excerpt from the *EPIC 2014* video:

> At its best, edited for the savviest readers, EPIC is a summary of the world – deeper, broader and more nuanced than anything ever available before – but at its worst, and for too many, EPIC is merely a collection of trivia, much of it untrue, all of it narrow, shallow and sensational. But EPIC is what we wanted, it's what we chose. And its commercial success preempted any discussion of media and democracy, or journalistic ethics.

That is why it's so important to know about what is happening, and to think critically about what it might mean. In terms of privacy, democracy and communication, blogging and social networking sites are changing our culture. While we live in democracies, are not in opposition to the government and abide by the law, the loss of privacy doesn't matter to us. It matters greatly in less democratic countries like China, where Yahoo! and Google have given data about individuals' searches to the government. It mattered to Hossein Derakhshan, a Canadian citizen whose blog was searched by immigration officers when he tried to enter the United States to go to a blogging conference. Derakhshan had spent a month in New York, staying at a friend's house, and had written in his blog that he was currently living in New York. The immigration officer took that literally – and as a Canadian citizen, Derakhshan had the right to visit the US for up to six months at a time, but not to take residence there. Derakshan was refused entry, but shared the story in his blog, *Editor: Myself*, on 24 November 2005.

Perhaps it is already too late to worry. We have, in a sense, already given up our privacy a long time ago. Margaret Atwood's book *The Handmaid's Tale* (1985) is set in a dystopic near-future North America where religious fundamentalism has led to extreme gender discrimination. Overnight, the government simply locks women's bank accounts so they cannot access their own money. Key cards to their workplaces stop working when the government decides that women should no longer have the right to work. During the Second World War, well before blogging or Google, the more detailed records a country kept of its population, the easier it was for Nazi invaders to persecute Jews and other groups. These acts of technologically assisted oppression were possible well before the Internet, Google or blogging.

Blogs and participatory media have both a liberatory potential, as is visible in the energy of the Iranian and Chinese blogosphere despite their governments' attempts to quash free speech, and a dangerous potential for increased surveillance and control. Blogs, knives and most other technologies can be used for good or for evil. If we're aware of how to use them and of how they are being used, we can help to shape the future.

References

Abrams, M. H. (1993) *A Glossary of Literary Terms*. Sixth edn. Fort Worth: Harcourt Brace.

acridrabbit et.al. (2001) 'Is it Possible that Kaycee Nicole Did Not Exist?', *Metafilter*, 18 May. Available from http://www.metafilter.com/comments.mefi/7819

Alerigi, Alberto. (2004) 'Brazil Internet Craze Angers English Speakers', *Yahoo! News*, 17 July. Was available from http://news.yahoo.com/news?tmpl=story&u=/nm/20040717/wr_nm/column_livewire_dc_1; use http://archive.org to access.

Anderson, Chris. (2006) *The Long Tail: Why the Future of Business is Selling Less of More*. New York: Hyperion.

Atwood, Margaret. (1985) *The Handmaid's Tale*. Toronto: McClelland and Stewart.

Bahnisch, Mark. (2006) 'The Political Uses of Blogs', in *Uses of Blogs*, edited by A. Bruns and J. Jacobs. New York: Peter Lang.

Baoill, Andrew Ó. (2004) 'Weblogs and the Public Sphere', in *Into the Blogosphere: Rhetoric, Community, and Culture of weblogs*, edited by L. Gurak, S. Antonijevic, L. Johnson, C. Ratliff and J. Reyman.

Baran, Paul. (1964) 'On Distributed Communications Networks', *Communications, IEEE Transactions* 12 (1): 1–9.

Bastiansen, Henrik Grue and Hans Fredrik Dahl. (2003) *Norsk mediehistorie*. Oslo: Universitetsforlaget.

bbc.co.uk. (2007) 'Blogging Ban for the Armed Forces', *BBC News*. http://news.bbc.co.uk/1/hi/uk/6940120.stm

Belson, Ken. (2006) 'Your Call Is Important to Us. Please Stay Awake', *New York Times*, 26 June. Available from http://www.nytimes.com/2006/06/26/technology/26comcast.html?

Benkler, Yochai. (2006) *The Wealth of Networks: How Social Production Transforms Markets and Freedom*. New Haven: Yale University Press.

Blogads. (2004) 'Reader Survey for Blog Advertising', available from http://www.blogads.com/survey/blog_reader_survey.html

Blood, Rebecca. (2000) 'Weblogs: A History and Perspective', *Rebecca's Pocket*. Available from http://www.rebeccablood.net/essays/weblog_history.html

Boeder, Pieter. (2005) 'Habermas' Heritage: The Future of the Public Sphere in the Network Society', *First Monday* 10 (9). Available from http://firstmonday.org/issues/issue10_9/boeder

Bolter, Jay David. (1991) *Writing Space: The Computer, Hypertext and the History of Writing*. First edn. Hove: Lawrence Erlbaum.

———— (2001) *Writing Space: Computers, Hypertext, and the Remediation of Print*. Second edn. Mahwah, NJ, and London: Lawrence Erlbaum Associates.

boyd, danah, and Jeffrey Heer. (2006) 'Profiles as Conversations: Networked Identity Performance on Friendster', paper read at Hawai'i International Conference on System Sciences, 4–7 January 2006, at Kauai, Hawai'i. Available from http://www.danah.org/papers/HICSS2006.pdf

boyd, danah. (2001) 'What's in a Name?', available at http://www.danah.org/name.html

———— (2007) 'Why Youth (Heart) Social Network Sites: The Role of Networked Publics in Teenage Social Life', in *Youth, Identity, and Digital Media*, edited by David Buckingham. Cambridge, MA: MIT Press.

Brecht, Bertolt. (1964) 'The Radio as an Apparatus of Communication', in *Brecht on Theatre*, edited by J. Willett. New York: Hill and Wang. (Original edition 1932).

Brooks, Peter. (1984) *Reading for the Plot: Design and Intention in Narrative*. Cambridge, MA: Harvard University Press.

Bruns, Axel. (2005) *Gatewatching: Collaborative Online News Production*. New York: Peter Lang.

Burke, Carolyn. n.d. About Carolyn's Diary. *The Online Diary History Project*. Available from http://www.diaryhistoryproject.com/recollections/1995_01_03.html

Bush, Vannevar. (1945) 'As We May Think', *Atlantic Monthly* 176 (1): 85–110.

Canham, Matt. (2006) 'Utah Blogger Makes her Life Public Fodder', *The Salt Lake Tribune*, 14 October.

Cantril, Hadley, Hazel Gaudet, and Herta Herzog. (1966) *The Invasion from Mars: A Study in the Psychology of Panic*. New York: Harper & Row. (Original edition 1940).

Castronova, Edward. (2005) *Synthetic Worlds: The Business and Culture of Online Games*. Chicago: University of Chicago Press.

Chandler, Daniel. (1996) 'Shaping and Being Shaped', *Computer-Mediated Communication Magazine* 3 (2). Available from http://www.december.com/cmc/mag/1996/feb/chandler.html

Chartier, Roger. (2001) 'The Practical Impact of Writing', in *The Book History Reader*, edited by D. Finkelstein and A. McCleery. London: Routledge.

Cook, Trevor. (2006) 'Can Blogging Unspin PR?', in *Uses of Blogs*, edited by Axel Bruns and Joanne Jacobs. New York: Peter Lang.

Crisell, Andrew. (2002) *An Introductory History of British Broadcasting*. London: Routledge.

Davis, Lloyd. (2006) 'Marketing and Selling Stormhoek Wines', *YouTube*. Available from http://www.youtube.com/watch?v=ODvfb37nR_4

Dean, Jodi. (2006) 'Blogging Theory', *Bad Subjects* 75. Available from http://bad.eserver.org/issues/2006/75/dean.htm

Doctorow, Cory. (2007) 'Scroogled', *Radar Online*. Available from http://www.radaronline.com/from-the-magazine/2007/09/google_fiction_evil_dangerous_surveillance_control_1.php

Doorframe (pseud.). (2006) 'Comcast Technician Sleeping on my Couch', *YouTube*. Available from http://www.youtube.com/watch?v=CvVp7b5gzqU

Douglas, J. Yellowlees. (2000) *The End of Books – or Books Without End? Reading Interactive Narratives*. Ann Arbor: The University of Michigan Press.

Edgecliffe-Johnson, Andrew. (2006) 'Web Use Overtakes Newspapers', 8 October. FT.com – *Financial Times*. Available from http://www.ft.com/cms/s/eb9509dc-5700-11db-9110-0000779e2340,_i_rssPage=6700d4e4-6714-11da-a650-0000779e2340.html

Eisenstein, Elizabeth. (1979) *The Printing Press as an Agent of Change: Communications and Cultural Transformations in Early-Modern Europe*. 2 vols. Vol. 1. Cambridge: Cambridge University Press.

Elatrash, Samer. (2007) 'Net Danger', *Montreal Mirror*. Available from http://www.montrealmirror.com/2007/070507/news1.html

Electronic Frontier Foundation. (2006) 'Apple v. Does', *Electronic Frontier Foundation*. Available from http://www.eff.org/Censorship/Apple_v_Does

Epstein, Michael. (1997) 'Licence', in *The Encyclopedia of Television*, edited by Horace Newcomb. Chicago: Fitzroy Dearborn Publishers. Also available from http://www.museum.tv/archives/etv

Faris, Michael. (2007) *Traversing the City of Blogs: Pedagogy, Performance, and Public Spheres*. MA thesis, Oregon State University. Available from http://oregonstate.edu/~farism/blog/wp-content/uploads/2007/10/faris-thesis-final-copy-complete.pdf

Fort, Caleb. (2005) 'CIRT blocks access to Facebook.com', *Daily Lobo*, 12 October. Available from http://media.www.dailylobo.com/media/storage/paper344/news/2005/10/12/News/Cirt-Blocks.Access.To.Facebook.com-1017983.shtml

Geitgey, Adam. (2001) 'The Kaycee Nicole (Swenson) FAQ Version 0.7.', Rootnode.org. Available from http://www.rootnode.org/article.php?sid=26

Gillespie, William, Scott Rettberg, Dirk Stratton and Frank Marquardt. (1998) *The Unknown*. Available from http://unknownhypertext.com

Glasner, Joanna. (2006) 'How to Almost Live on Blogging', *Wired*, 2 February. Available from http://www.wired.com/science/discoveries/news/2006/02/70161

Gogoi, Pallavi. (2006) 'Wal-Mart's Jim and Laura: The Real Story', *Business Week*, 8 October. Available from http://www.businessweek.com/bwdaily/dnflash/content/oct2006/db20061009_579137.htm?campaign_id=rss_topStories_msnbc

Granovetter, Mark. (1973) 'The Strength of Weak Ties', *The American Journal of Sociology* 78 (6): 1360–80.

Griffin, Christopher. (2007) 'Internet Insecurity', *Armed Forces Journal*. Available from http://www.armedforcesjournal.com/2007/06/2740192

Habermas, Jürgen. (1991) *The Structural Transformation of the Public Sphere: An Inquiry into a Category of Bourgeois Society*. Cambridge, MA: MIT Press. Original edition, 1962.

——— (2006) 'Towards a United States of Europe', *Signandsight.com*. Available from http://www.signandsight.com/features/676.html

Hall, Justin. (2004) *Justin's Links*. Available from http://links.net

——— (2005) 'Darknight.mov' *Justin's Links*. Available from http://www.links.net/daze/05/01/pix/darknight.mov

Hayles, N. Katherine. (2007) 'Electronic Literature: What is It?', The Electronic Literature Organization. Available from http://eliterature.org/pad/elp.html

Heffernan, Virginia. (2006) ' "Lonely Girl" (and Friends) Just Wanted Movie Deal', *New York Times*, 12 September. Available from http://www.nytimes.com/2006/09/12/technology/12cnd-lonely.html

Herring, Susan C., Inna Kouper, Lois Ann Scheidt, and Elijah L. Wright. (2004) 'Women and Children Last: The Discursive Construction of "Weblogs" ', in *Into the Blogosphere: Rhetoric, Community, and Culture of Weblogs*, edited by L. Gurak, S. Antonijevic, L. Johnson,

C. Ratliff and J. Reyman. Available from http://blog.lib.umn.edu/blogosphere/women_and_children.html

Hiler, John. (2002) 'The Date Project', *Microcontent News*, 30 October. Was available from http://www.microcontentnews.com/entries/20021030-1892.htm; use http://archive.org to access.

Iser, Wolfgang. (1988) 'The Reading Process: A Phenomenological Approach', in *Modern Criticism and Theory: A Reader*, edited by David Lodge. London: Longman.

Johnson, Steven. (2005) *Everything Bad is Good for You: How Today's Popular Culture is Actually Making Us Smarter*. New York: Riverhead Books.

Joyce, Michael. (1990) *afternoon, a story*. Cambridge, MA: Eastgate Systems.

Keren, Michael. (2006) *Blogosphere: The New Political Arena*. Plymouth: Lexington Books.

Knights, Mark. (2005) *Representation and Misrepresentation in Later Stuart Britain: Partisanship and Political Culture*. Oxford: Oxford University Press.

Kozinets, Robert. (2006) 'Netnography 2.0.', in *Handbook of Qualitative Research Methods in Marketing*, edited by Russell W. Belk. Cheltenham: Edward Elgar Publishing.

Lanham, Richard A. (1993) *The Electronic Word: Democracy, Technology, and the Arts*. Chicago: University of Chicago Press.

Lasica, J. D. (2003) 'Blogs and Journalism Need Each Other', available from http://www.nieman.harvard.edu/reports/03-3NRfall/V57 N3.pdf
——— (2005) 'The Cost of Ethics: Influence Peddling in the Blogosphere', *USC Annenberg Online Journalism Review*. Available from http://www.ojr.org/ojr/stories/050217lasica

Lejeune, Phillippe. (2001) 'How do Diaries End?', *Biography* 24 (1): 99–112.

Lenhart, Amanda, and Susannah Fox. (2006) 'Bloggers: A Portrait of the Internet's New Storytellers', Washington, DC: Pew Internet and American Life Project. Available from http://207.21.232.103/PPF/r/186/report_display.asp

Lessig, Lawrence. (2004) *Free Culture: How Big Media Uses Technology and the Law to Lock Down Culture and Control Creativity*. New York: Penguin.

Liebling, Abbott Joseph. (1960) 'Do You Belong in Journalism?', *New Yorker*, 14 May.

Lovink, Geert. (2007a) 'Blogging: The Nihilist Impulse', *Eurozine*. Available from http://www.eurozine.com/articles/2007-01-02-lovink-en.html

———— (2007b) *Zero Comments: Blogging and Critical Internet Culture.* New York: Taylor and Francis.

Matrullo, Tom. (2002) 'Loci Amoeni', *Commonplaces*, 21 January. Available from http://tom.weblogs.com/discuss/msgReader$786

McConnell, Ben and Jackie Huba. (2007) *Citizen Marketers: When People are the Message.* Chicago: Kaplan Publishing.

McLuhan, Marshall. (1962) *The Gutenberg Galaxy: The Making of Typographical Man.* Toronto: University of Toronto Press.

———— (1977) 'The Laws of the Media', *Et cetera* 34 (2): 173–9.

Mead, Rebecca. (2006) 'Meg and Jason', *New Yorker*, 6 June. Available from http://www.newyorker.com/archive/2006/06/05 /060605 ta_talk_mead

Milgram, Stanley. (1967) 'The Small World Problem', *Psychology Today* 1: 61–7.

Miller, Carolyn R., and Dawn Shepherd. (2004) 'Blogging as Social Action: A Genre Analysis of the Weblog', in *Into the Blogosphere: Rhetoric, Community, and Culture of Weblogs*, edited by L. Gurak, S. Antonijevic, L. Johnson, C. Ratliff and J. Reyman. Available from http://blog.lib.umn.edu/blogosphere/blogging_as_social_action_a _genre_analysis_of_the_weblog.html

Mookerjee, Vijay, and Milind Dawande. (2007) 'In 2006, the Top 50K Blogs Generated $500M in Ad Revenue', University of Texas/Chitika. Available from http://chitika.com/blogdollar /UTDallas-Chitika-BlogDollar-Research-Report-FullVersion.pdf

Moulthrop, Stuart. (1991) 'You Say you Want a Revolution? Hypertext and the Laws of Media', *Postmodern Culture* 1 (3). Available from muse. jhu.edu/journals/postmodern_culture/v001/1.3moulthrop.html

National Endowment for the Arts. (2004) 'Reading at Risk: A Survey of Literary Reading in America', Washington, DC. Available from http://www.nea.gov/news/news04/ReadingAtRisk.html

Nelson, Theodore H. (1965) 'A File Structure for the Complex, the Changing, and the Indeterminate', *Association for Computing Machinery: Proc. 20th National Conference*, 84–100.

———— (1970) 'No More Teachers' Dirty Looks', *Computer Decisions* 9 (8): 16–23.

———— (1974) *Computer Lib/Dream Machine.* Self-published.

———— (1993) *Literary Machines 93: This Book Describes the Legendary and Daring Project Xanadu, an Initiative Toward an Instantaneous Electronic Literature.* Sausalito CA: Mindful Press.

Nielsen, Jakob. (1997) 'How Users Read on the Web', *Useit.com: Alertbox*, 1 October. Available from http://www.useit.com/ alertbox/9710a.html

Notaro, Anna. (2006) 'The Lo(n)g Revolution: The Blogosphere as an Alternative Public Sphere?', *Reconstruction* 6 (4). Available from http://reconstruction.eserver.org/064/notaro.shtml.

Ong, Walter J. (1982) *Orality and Literacy: The Technologizing of the Word.* London: Routledge.

O'Reilly, Tim. (2005) 'What is Web 2.0? Design Patterns and Business Models for the Next Generation of Software', *Oreilly.com.* 30 September. Available from http://www.oreilly.com/pub/a/oreilly/tim/news/2005/09/30/what-is-Web-20.html

Peters, John Durham. (1999) *Speaking Into the Air: A History of the Idea of Communication.* Chicago: University of Chicago Press.

Pettitt, Tom. (2007) 'Before the Gutenberg Parenthesis: Elizabethan–American Compatibility', Plenary lecture given at Media in Transition 5: Creativity, Ownership and Collaboration in the Digital Age. Cambridge, MA: Massachusetts Institute of Technology, 27–29 April. Available from http://Web.mit.edu/comm-forum/mit5/papers/pettitt_plenary_gutenberg.pdf

Plato. (1999) *Phaedrus.* Translated by Benjamin Jowett. Champaign, Illinois: Project Gutenberg. Orig. about 360 BC. Available from http://www.gutenberg.org/etext/1636

Poster, Mark. (1997) 'Cyberdemocracy: Internet and the Public Sphere', in *Internet Culture*, edited by D. Porter. New York: Routledge.

Powazek, Derek. (2001) 'A Conversation With my Sister', *The Life and Times of Derek M. Powazek, Real Person*, 20 May. Available from http://www.powazek.com/zoom/log/archive/00000058.shtml

Rainie, Lee. (2005) 'The State of Blogging', Washington DC: Internet & American Life Project. Available from http://www.pewinternet.org/report_display.asp?r=144

Rich, Cindy. (2007) 'Secret Life of Teens: Facebook – The Trouble with Facebook', *Washingtonian.com*, 1 August. Available from http://www.washingtonian.com/articles/education/4938.html

Robinett, Paul (a.k.a. Renetto). (2006) 'LonelyGirl15 is a FAKE . . . PLEASE WATCH!!!', *YouTube.* Available from http://www.youtube.com/watch?v=z05X9nNNXLU&NR

Rowse, Darren. (2007) 'How Much Money Do Bloggers Earn Blogging?', *ProBlogger*, 30 November. Available from http://www.problogger.net/archives/2007/11/30/how-much-money-do-bloggers-earn-blogging

Ryan, Marie-Laure. (2005) 'Media and Narrative', in *Routledge Encyclopedia of Narrative Theory*, edited by David Herman, Manfred Jahn and Marie-Laure Ryan. London and New York: Routledge.

Scoble, Robert, and Shel Israel. (2006) *Naked Conversations: How Blogs Are Changing the Way Businesses Talk with Customers*. Hoboken, NJ: Wiley.

Sennett, Richard. (1986) *The Fall of Public Man*. London: Faber and Faber.

Serfaty, Viviane. (2004) *The Mirror and the Veil: An Overview of American Online Diaries and Blogs*. Amsterdam: Amsterdam Monographs in American Studies.

Shirky, Clay. (2003) 'Power Laws, Weblogs, and Inequality', *Clay Shirky's Writings about the Internet: Economics & Culture, Media & Community, Open Source*. Available from http://www.shirky.com/writings/powerlaw/powerlaw_weblog.html

Sifry, David. (2007) 'The State of the Live Web, April 2007', *Sifry's Alerts*. Available from http://www.sifry.com/alerts/archives/000493.html

Sloan, Robin and Matt Thompson. (2004) *EPIC 2014*. Available from http://www.robinsloan.com/epic

Statistics Norway. (2007) 'Norwegian Media Barometer 2006', available from http://www.ssb.no/medie_en

Thomas, Angela. (2006) 'Fictional Blogging', in *Uses of Blogs*, edited by A. Bruns and J. Jacobs. New York: Peter Lang.

Turnball, Giles. (2001) 'The State of the Blog. Interview with Evan Williams', *Write the Web*. Available from http://writetheWeb.com/Members/gilest/old/108

US Census Bureau. (2006) 'Statistical Abstract of the United States: 2007', available from http://www.census.gov/prod/www/statistical-abstract.html

US Congress. House. *Free Flow of Information Act of 2005*. HR-3323. 109th Cong., 1st sess.

US Congress. House. *Free Flow of Information Act of 2006*. S. 2831. 109th Cong., 2nd sess.

Walker Art Center. (2006) 'Walker Blog Guidelines', *New Media Iniatives Blog*, 9 March. http://blogs.walkerart.org/newmedia/2006/03/09/walker-blog-guidlines/

Walker, Jill. (2005a) 'Weblog', in *Routledge Encyclopedia of Narrative Theory*, edited by David Herman, Manfred Jahn and Marie-Laure Ryan. London and New York: Routledge.

——— (2005b) 'Feral Hypertext: When Hypertext Literature Escapes Control', in *Proceedings of ACM Hypertext 2005*. Salzburg, 6–9 September. Available from http://jilltxt.net/txt/FeralHypertext.pdf

Wall, Melissa. (2005) ' "Blogs of War": Weblogs as News', *Journalism* 6 (2): 153–72.

Wardrip-Fruin, Noah. (2004) 'What Hypertext Is', *Proceedings of ACM Hypertext 2004*. Santa Cruz, CA, 9–13 August. Available from http://portal.acm.org/citation.cfm?doid=1012807.1012844

Weinberger, David. (2002) *Small Pieces Loosely Joined: A Unified Theory of the Web*. Cambridge, MA: Perseus.

Wittig, Rob. (2003) 'Justin Hall and the Birth of the 'Blogs', *Electronic Book Review*. Available from http://www.electronicbookreview. com/ thread/electropoetics/serial

Woning, Randall van der. (2001) 'The End of the Whole Mess', available from http://bigwhiteguy.com/mess.shtml

Wright, Jeremy. (2005) *Blog Marketing: The Revolutionary New Method to Increase Sales, Growth, and Profits*. New York: McGraw-Hill.

Blogs Mentioned

A Little Pregnant. 2003–present. Julie. http://www.alittlepregnant.com

Apophenia. 1997–present. danah boyd. http://www.zephoria.org/thoughts

Arla weblogs. 2005–present. Maja Møller, Jacob Nørgård, Tove Færch, Inge and Mikael Nørby Lassen. http://arla.dk/weblogs

Ars Technica. 1998–present. Ken Fisher (ed.). http://arstechnica.com

A Whole Lotta Nothing. 2000–present. Matt Haughey. http://a.wholelottanothing.org

Barbie. 2002–2003. Mattel, Inc. http://www.myscene.com/barbie/barbie_index.asp (no longer online; use http://archive.org to access)

Barq's – the Blog with BITE! 2005–2007. http://thebarqsman.com

BlogWrite for CEOs. 2004–present. Debbie Weil. http://www.blogwriteforceos.com

Boing Boing: A Directory of Wonderful Things. 2000–present. Mark Frauenfelder, Cory Doctorow, Xeni Jardin, Joel Johnson, John Battelle, David Pescovitz. http://boingboing.net

Brooklyn Tweed. 2005–present. Jared Flood. http://brooklyntweed.blogspot.com

Chronicles of Dr. Crazy. 2006. Dr. Crazy (pseud.). http://crazyphd.blogspot.com

ClickNews! 2006–present. Lynn Terry. http://www.clicknewz.com

Daily Kos. 2002–present. Markos Moulitsas (publisher/founder). http://dailykos.com

Digital Photography Blog. 2004–present. Darren Rowse. http://www.livingroom.org.au/photolog

Dooce. 2001–present. Heather B. Armstrong. http://dooce.com

Editor: Myself. A Weblog on Iran, Technology and Pop Culture. 2002–2007. Hossein Derakhshan. http://hoder. com/weblog

Engadget. 2004–present. Peter Rojas (ed.). http://engadget.com

ExperienceCurve. 2003–present. Karl Long. http:// experiencecurve.com

GapingVoid. 2004–present. Hugh MacLeod. http://gapingvoid.com

Get Real. 2003–2006. Steve Boyd. http://getreal.corante.com

Get Rich Slowly. 2006–present. J. D. Roth. http://www.getrichslowly. org/blog

Gizmodo. 2002–present. Brian Lam (ed.). http://gizmodo.com

GrandTextAuto. 2003–present. Mary Flanagan, Michael Mateas, Nick Montfort, Scott Rettberg, Andrew Stern and Noah Wardrip-Fruin. http://grandtextauto.org

jill/txt. 2000–present. Jill Walker Rettberg. http://jilltxt.net

Klastrup's Cataclysms. 2001–present. Lisbeth Klastrup. http://klastrup.dk

Kottke.org. 1998–present. Jason Kottke. http://kottke.org

KottkeKomments. http://kottkekomments.com

Kuro5hin. 1999–present. Rusty Foster (founder). http://www. kuro5hin.org

LifeHack. 2005–present. Leon Ho (ed.). http://lifehack.org

Links.net. 1994–2005. Justin Hall. http://links.net

Lonelygirl15. 2006–present. Miles Beckett, Ramesh Flinders et.al. http://lonelygirl15.com

Matt Cutts: Gadgets, Google, and SEO. 2005–present. Matt Cutts. http://www.mattcutts.com/blog

Manolo's Shoe Blog. 2004–present. Manolo (pseud.). http:// shoeblogs.com

MegNut. 1999–present. Meg Hourihan. http://megnut.com

Metafilter. 1999–present. Matt Haughey (ed.). http://metafilter.com

Molly.com. 2003–present. Molly Holzschlag. http://molly.com

MotherTalkers. 2006–present. Amy, Elisa, Erika and Gloria. http:// mothertalkers.com

Mr Smash Goes to Washington. Mr Smash (pseud.). Blog previously titled *Citizen Smash, Lt. Smash, Indepundit.* 2003–2006. http://lt-smash.com [no longer available]

MSTechToday. Unknown–2007. Brandon LeBlanc. http://mstech today.com [no longer available]

Narcissism, vanity, exhibitionism, ambition, vanity, vanity, vanity. 2001–present. Diane Greco. http://home.earthlink.net/~dianegreco

ntcoolfool. 2006–2007. Bryce Carter. http://ntcoolfool. livejournal.com

O'Reilly Radar. 2005–present. Tim O'Reilly et.al. http://radar.oreilly.com

PeterMe. 1998–present. Peter Merholz. http://peterme.com

PostSecret. 2004–present. Frank Warren (ed.). http://postsecret.com

ProBlogger. 2004–present. Darren Rowse. http://problogger.com

Read/Write Web. 2003–present. Richard MacManus (ed.). http://www. readwriteWeb.com

Rebecca's Pocket. 1999–present. Rebecca Blood. http://www.rebecca blood.net

Robot Wisdom. 1997–present. Jorn Barger. http://robotwisdom.com

Scripting News. 1997–present. Dave Winer. http://scripting.com

She's a Flight Risk. 2003–2006. Isabella K. (pseud.). http://shes. aflightrisk.org; no longer online; use http://archive.org to access.

Shiny Shiny. 2003–present. Katie Lee (ed.). http://shinyshiny.tv

Slashdot. 1997–present. Rob 'Cmdr Taco' Malda, Jeff 'Hemos' Bates, Robin 'Roblimo' Miller (eds.). http://slashdot.org

Stormhoek. 2005–present. Hugh MacLeod et.al. http:// stormhoek.com

Style Bytes. 2005–present. Agathe Bjørnsdatter. http://stylebytes.net

Tales of a Bathroom Scale. Lori. 2002–2003. http://dietchick.blogspot. com

Tama Leaver dot Net. 2007–present. Tama Leaver. http://tamaleaver.net

TechCrunch. 2005–2007. Michael Arrington (ed.). http:// techcrunch.com

techPresident. 2007–present. Micah Sifry and Joshua Levy (eds.). http://techpresident.com

The Date Project. 2002. Anonymous. http://thedateproject.blogspot. com (URL since taken over by another blogger; use http:// archive.org to access original blog)

The Dullest Blog in the World. 2003–2006. Anonymous. http:// www.wibsite.com/wiblog/dull

The English Cut. 2005–present. Thomas Mahon. http://www.english cut.com

The Quantum Pontiff. 2003–present. Dave Beacon. http://science blogs.com/pontiff

The Viral Garden. 2005–present. Mark Collier. http://moblogsmo problems.blogspot.com

Wal-Marting Across America. 2006. Laura. http://walmartin gacrossamerica.com

We're in Debt. 2006–present. King and Queen of Debt (pseud.). http://wereindebt.com

Where is Raed? 2003–2004. Salam Pax (pseud.). http:// dear_raed.blogspot.com

Index